Fly-Fishing Inshore Saltwaters for Pacific Salmon

Science-Based Innovation for the Practical Fly-Fisher

Richard K. Stoll

Fly-Fishing Inshore Saltwaters for Pacific Salmon

Science-Based Innovation for the Practical Fly-Fisher

Richard K. Stoll

Frank Amato
Publications

All inquiries should be addressed to:
Frank Amato Publications, Inc. • P.O. Box 82112 • Portland, Oregon 97282
503-653-8108 • www.AmatoBooks.com

Book and Cover Design by Mariah Hinds
Photography by Richard K. Stoll unless otherwise noted
Appendix I Illustrations provided by Washington Department of Fish and Wildlife

ISBN-10: 1-57188-486-6
ISBN-13: 978-1-57188-486-2
UPC: 0-81127-00331-0

Printed in China

Table of Contents

Acknowledgements

I retain responsibility for the contents herein, some of which challenges angling status quo based on how I interpret scientific literature on Pacific salmon.

Having stated this I am grateful to fly-angling friends, fellow anglers, my former fly fishing shop clients and those I have had the privilege to fish with over the years. I learned an immeasurable amount from our personal interactions both on the water and off. These people are too numerous to mention here. However, there are a few who stand out. Special thanks to Ted Teather and Bill Drewry of Peninsula Outfitters, and Leland Miyawaki, Manager of the Orvis store fishing department in Bellevue, Washington. Their comments and photographic contributions helped me to gain valuable perspectives and better communicate my ideas. I am grateful to my former fly fishing shop partner, Bob Searle, a very creative fly designer and fly angler. I learned a lot from Bob. Bob now owns Pacific Coast Anglers Travel Adventures (www.pcatraveladventures.com). I am also particularly grateful to Bill Thompson, former National Geographic photographer and adventurer, for his assistance and advice on how to deal with my pictures and graphics.

The many special persons I see and fish with on a regular basis have also contributed in so many ways they do not realize. These include Mark Salo, longtime friend and fishing partner, Jim Russell, Dick Larson, and Bob Walling, among others.

Without the above individuals, the creation of this book would not have been possible.

Introduction

It was over twenty years ago when I first recognized the enormous fly fishing potential for salmon along the beaches and in the estuaries and bays of Puget Sound. At the time I was an owner of Northwest Angler, a fly fishing store in Poulsbo, Washington. I was also the weekly fishing columnist for several local newspapers. My shop was located in the western Puget Sound area just a few miles north of the Sage fly rod factory. We had marginal lake fishing for hatchery trout, nearly non-existent stream fishing, and a largely unexplored but excellent sea run cutthroat fishery. Spring through fall we would shuttle out clients off to lakes east of the Cascade Mountains, over a hundred miles away. For the more hardy souls willing to hike rivers, wade deep, and sometimes make numerous trips without a fish, we recommended the brawling Pacific Northwest salmon and steelhead rivers. Like all good purveyors of the sport, I was interested sharing good local fisheries with my customers and the readers of my weekly newspaper columns. You know, those were the local places to go Saturday morning or after work on long summer eves. But I was also painfully aware that one can only send so many people to sea-run cutthroat heaven before it was heaven no longer.

Largely because of Les Johnson and Bruce Ferguson's 1985 book, *Fly Fishing for Pacific Salmon*, several of us started exploring local beaches in hopes of tying into something rather larger than cutthroat. One of our prime targets was the white sand beach at Point no Point, some 15 miles north of my shop. Point no Point was long famous as a plug-cut herring boat fishery. Both Chinook and Coho would hand on a very pronounced underwater bar a hundred yards offshore. However, it was no secret that Coho salmon were sometimes being taken very close to the point's white sandy beach. It did not take us beach-bound anglers long to discover there was wonderful summer through fall salmon fly fishing from beaches right at our back door.

During the same period some of the more elite of the Pacific fly-angling community started catching freight-train Chum salmon off the mouth of Finch Creek in the southern Hood Canal. This October to November fishery came on just after the Coho runs petered out. We discovered other easily accessible Chum runs in a number of estuaries close to home. One of these was the Chico Creek estuary, some 15 minutes south of my shop. I started writing about both the Coho and Chum fisheries in my weekly columns and enthusiastically talked about them to my friends and clients. Point no Point,

Finch Creek and Chico Creek soon became quite popular fly-angling destinations as they continue to be today.

Over the intervening years my angling acquaintances and I have spent a lot of time wandering beaches and rummaging around estuaries, bays and river mouths in search of new locations and more effective ways to catch salmon on a fly rod. As a professional biologist I also started looking at salmon behavior from a scientific point of view. I combed scientific literature and made some interesting discoveries on how and why salmon act, interact, and react the way they do. The observations in this book reflect the current state of my investigations.

For some fly anglers, including myself, fly fishing is far more than hooking and playing a fish. Rather, it is engagement with the totality of the environments that support fish. This is what this book is about, that is looking beyond rods, reels, lines, leaders and the functional aspects of fly fishing solely targeted at catching fish.

I share my perspectives as to the whys and wherefores of the behaviors of salmon and their prey. I put forward new ways of looking at fly-angling for Pacific salmon, and indeed fly-angling in general. The fishing methods and fly designs contained herein embrace experience, science, technology and tradition. In some cases they even challenge some of the most common fly-angling conventions. For example, most modern fly patterns and angling methods are based on human perception. Anglers often make assumptions that fish see and react like humans. They transpose these into how they design flies and how they fish these flies. However, the way salmon and other fishes respond to prey is often far different than we fly anglers may perceive.

I have been long intrigued by a number of questions. When and how do salmon eat? What are the best fly colors? Why does fluorescent chartreuse sometimes work so well? How much action should a fly have? Is fly silhouette a significant factor? When and under what conditions do salmon most actively take a fly? Do adult salmon stop feeding before they enter a stream to spawn?

Understanding of the complex biological and physical patterns of nature and how both salmon and their prey behave and interact can enable us to come closer to answering these questions. Reasoned and researched answers necessarily lead to more successful fly designs and a better understanding of how and when to use them. In turn your fly-angling experience can be more successful and pleasurable.

*Whale Passage, Prince of Wales Island can provide
some spectacular July Coho fishing.*

Many of my observations have been drawn from angling adventures in the waters of Puget Sound. I also draw from my many fishing experiences in Alaska and British Columbia. The observations I have made apply to the full geographic range of all Pacific salmon runs around the Pacific Rim, from Russia to California. However, it must be recognized there is a great deal of variability in nature. Therefore, these observations will often vary to some degree for specific locations, situations, and specific salmon runs.

Saltwater fly fishing is just as complex and involved in different ways as other types of fly fishing. Salt waters are like rivers. Both exhibit their own

The beautiful Pasagschak River estuary is located about 25 miles south of the town of Kodiak on paved road. Returning Sockeye salmon are prolific late July to early August. In late September to early October numerous returning Coho salmon average approximately fourteen to fifteen pounds, with some fish running well in excess of eighteen pounds. This makes the Pasagschak one of the largest average-size Coho runs anywhere.

*My salmon fishing friends sharing fishing stories at our weekly
Monday coffee clatch at Peninsula Outfitters in Poulsbo, WA.
Left to Right: Dick Larson, Ted Teather, Bob Walling.*

unique characteristics. They are burdened to the same physical forces that
influence the adaptive nature of the species that inhabit them. Traditionally,
fly anglers have attuned themselves to rivers and streams with all the
complex anomalies related to fishing these types of waters. But there are
lifetimes of dedication and study in saltwater fly-angling that have not yet
been ventured into.

A limited number of scientific papers have been cited to substantiate my
findings. It should be recognized the scientific literature on salmon behavior
including color perception, feeding habits, and sound perception among
other pertinent issues is voluminous, complex, and sometimes may even
appear to be contradictory. For those who wish, further exploration can be
accomplished following the train of bibliographical citations cited in each of
the respective references at the end of this book.

The last chapter contains commentary on the environmental challenges
that affect the future of our salmon fisheries. Salmon are fast succumbing to

Paul Stoll

The author waiting for the tide to set up on a Puget Sound point. The best times to fish salmon from a beach are when the tide sets up during early mornings and late evenings. Note the tide rip approximately 100 feet out from the beach.

the onslaught of western growth-oriented economics. This is the result of ever-increasing and unsustainable demand for natural resources in pursuit of wealth. Fly anglers can better work to preserve our fishing resources with a modicum of understanding of some of the factors that contribute to the decline of our fisheries. We cannot continue to deplete the world's natural resources and still expect to keep the precious outdoor amenities that support healthy fish populations.

Fly-angling in general is a unique sport in that it necessarily spawns an intimate interaction with nature. This is what the following pages are about, interaction with nature. As such fly-angling engenders an environmental sensitivity in ways that we can be part of the forces for preservation of all fish populations, but particularly salmon populations. It is, in large part, up to each of us to become an activist for the sport and the resources we love. As Henry David Thoreau once stated; *"In the Wilderness is the Preservation of the World."*

Enjoy!

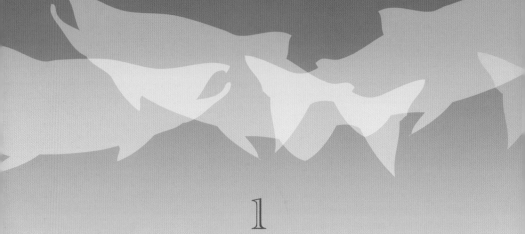

1

Understanding the Underwater World of Pacific Salmon

"Following the period of grace and gratitude for the harvests of summer's bounty the world moves into its winter cycle and life moves with it. It is a time when darkness comes sooner and stays longer; when nothing grows very fast. It is a time when salmon are moving to fall spawning grounds to become a greater part of the cycle of nature. The gravelly crypts of salmon parents form the fetal wombs of a new generation of sea-bound fish. The bodies of the deceased will provide nutrients for the spring emergence of their newborn progeny."

—Stoll, 2003

Imagine the world salmon live in. This is a world where salmon can move in any direction, up, down, forward, or to the side. Their world is composed of a collage of low-frequency sound, smells, and muted light. The seascape is punctuated by blue, green and gray tones with some muted other colors in shallow waters. Often what salmon see is silhouetted against the blues and grays of either the sky or the backdrop of surrounding waters. They live in a soup of chemicals, other fish and invertebrates, marine mammals, plankton, and whatever man discards to the ocean. Salmon live in and therefore perceive their environment in very much different ways than we humans perceive and live in ours.

The underwater environment is profoundly different than the air environment. Light and color not only attenuate faster but take on different characteristics in aquatic environments. Sound travels faster and further while maintaining higher intensities over distance in water than in air. Underwater environments are characterized to a large degree by currents, waves, vibrations and water movements. Likewise, underwater organisms are uniquely adapted to respond to these aquatic characteristics, fish included.

Fish are adapted to see light and color in very unique ways. Their bodies are greatly adapted to perceiving sound and subsonic sound-like waves with both inner ears and lateral lines that extend the full length of their bodies. Fish can virtually "see" to a highly sophisticate degree without sight. Because these sense organs are bilateral they have the ability to perceive depth, direction, and intensity. During dark hours and in deep waters many species of fish can effectively feed without the ability to see clearly, if at all. With relatively minor variations visual/audio senses are nearly identical in all salmonids species, trout included.

Conversely, we anglers are often so anthropocentric as to think that fish respond to the same things in the same ways in their aquatic environment as we do in our air environment. We design and fish our flies the way we think fish see them, which is actually the way we see them. We substantially ignore other perception factors that motivate fish to behave as they do as a function of survival in their underwater world.

Great and wonderful books have been written on the presupposed finite details of fish perception. Most have been about trout and other fish species (Kageyama, 1999; Ross, 2000;...). In 1971 Doug Swisher and Bruce Richards looked at dry-fly profiles from underwater in *Selective Trout*. In 1973 Ernie Schweibert studied the utmost physical detail of major species of mayflies in *Nymphs*. In 1976 Vince Marinaro described trout feeding behavior in *The Ring of the Rise*. Most recently, in 2010 Arlen Thomason explored aquatic insect life in *Bugwater* with a series of spectacular photographs. None that I know of take a comprehensive look at how salmonids interact with their environment from their physiological and ethological perspectives, and considering the physics of color, light, and currents in water. This book attempts to fill these gaps to some degree.

There are five primary species of salmon on the west coast of mainland USA, Canada, and Alaska. These are Chinook salmon, Coho salmon, Chum salmon, Pink salmon, and Sockeye salmon. Appendix I contains detailed characteristics of their ranges, life history and habits.

Each salmon of these salmon species is not only unique in and of itself, but unique within their native runs for any particular river system. Wild salmon have fundamentally adapted to both the specific watersheds they spawn and rear in. Likewise, they are adapted to the saltwater areas they migrate to for the majority of their lives. Anglers and commercial fishermen have long noticed differences in specific salmon runs including size, shape, coloration, where, when, and how they run, and even how they may respond to bait, lures and flies.

Genetic dilution by hatchery salmon has muted the differences between salmon runs. According to many biologists and anglers alike this has not been for the better. The dilution of gene pools adapted to unique watersheds and attendant environmental conditions has affected the ability of many salmon runs to successfully spawn. Successful spawning is the production of progeny that produce offspring that return to successfully spawn themselves in adequate numbers to maintain their runs.

Saltwater fly anglers most commonly target four salmon life stages. These are in-migrating adult salmon, feeder salmon, terminal salmon, and resident salmon. It is relatively

A nice resident Chinook salmon taken off a Puget Sound beach. The adipose fin is clipped indicating this is a late-release hatchery fish.

uncommon that fly anglers target salmon in the open ocean except in special locations like the mouth of the Straights of San Juan de Fuca during the July-August in-migrating Coho runs. Salmon are most commonly accessible to fly anglers as in-migrating adults along points and beaches, as resident juveniles, and as terminal estuarine populations.

Resident salmon stay in inshore salt waters throughout their entire life rather than making lengthy sea migrations. Some proportion of both juvenile Chinook salmon and Coho salmon populations do not migrate to sea. Rather they become permanent residents in sounds, bays and inlets. Today the majority of these resident fish are of hatchery origin. In the Puget Sound, resident Coho fisheries are supplemented by agencies like the Washington State Department of Fish and Wildlife by holding the young Coho in net pens longer than usual. This causes a large portion to remain in the Puget Sound. Puget Sound resident Coho will often make a mini migration north into the Straits of Juan de Fuca, but do not general grow as large as their ocean-going counterparts. The same is true of resident Chinook salmon commonly called blackmouth by Puget Sound anglers. These are also artificially supplemented with late-release hatchery fish. Both resident Chinook and Coho can be found in estuaries, bays and inlets from Oregon to Alaska.

Ted Teather

Coho Salmon on a bed of eel grass. Contrary to common belief, eel grass is not a sea weed but a perennial grass.

Unique salmon sense and behavioral attributes discussed in this book have three primary purposes. These are feeding, avoiding predators, and spawning. Understanding how salmon perceive their environment and attendant behaviors should be of great interest to fly anglers, especially those who design flies. With regard to salmon behavior I think nine fundamental questions need to be addressed.

① What do salmon see?

② Do salmon see color?

③ How do silhouette, contrast, and color interact in salmon feeding behavior?

④ What is the importance of fluorescence and flash in salmon feeding behavior?

⑤ Does the lateral line have a function in salmon feeding behavior?

⑥ What effect does smell have on salmon feeding behavior?

⑦ How do salmon respond to sound?

⑧ When and under what conditions do Salmon most actively feed?

⑨ Why do returning salmon jump?

Each of these questions is discussed below.

What Do Salmon See?

Visual Acuity

Scientific studies of fish eyes show that the majority of species see a relatively focused image, detect motion, and have relatively good contrast-detection ability. This also appears to be generally true of salmonids. However, because of the shape of the salmon eye, salmon do not appear to have vision as acute as humans. They do not see fine detail nor do they need to in their environment. Rather, they see shapes and size, and they can discern and respond to prey movement. Perception of movement is complemented by the lateral line senses described in item 4 below. Therefore, attention to finite fly-design detail is not as important for the fish as it is for the angler.

Polarization

Salmon eyes polarize light. Polarization reduces light scatter. Anglers know the beneficial effects of polarized lenses when observing what is below water surface. For salmon, polarization may enhance their ability to recognize bait against dark backgrounds, in darker conditions, and further away. As a consideration in fly design the ability of salmon eyes to polarize light may also enhance their perception of flash such as that made by fleeing baitfish.

Field of Vision

A salmon's field of vision is considerably wider than a human's. Salmon eyes are also quite mobile. Salmon can move their eyes to expand their field of vision. However, the position of their eyes, the shape of their head and mouth parts, the ovular shape of the eye, and the angle of impingement on the retina create a large rear and down-looking blind spot. There is also a blind spot directly in front of a salmon. Their visual axis is forward and up. Depth perception is possible forward and up when the field of view is in both eyes. There is little or no depth perception to the sides where the field of vision is by only one eye. This is significant for the fly angler in that it is most effective to present a fly in front of, or above, a fish.

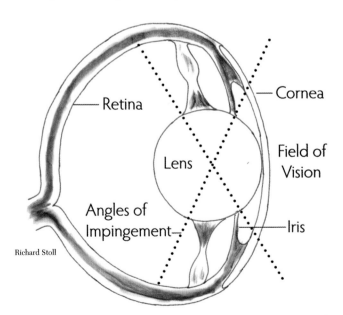

The fish eye is more of a flattened oval than the human eye. This may reduce focal acuity. In addition, the angles of light impingement on the retina are one of the factors that restrict field of vision.

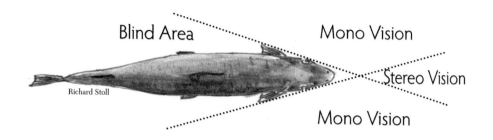

Blind Area   Mono Vision

Richard Stoll

Stereo Vision

Mono Vision

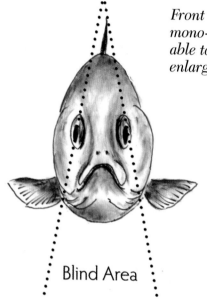

Blind Area

Front and top views of stereo-vision, mono-vision, and blind areas. Salmon are able to rotate their eyes which make these enlarged fields of vision possible.

Snell's Window

Salmon view the outside world through a round window in the surface of the water. The diameter of this window is a little more than twice the depth of the fish. Beyond the edges of this window, light is reflected off the under surface of the water. The underside of the surface of the water becomes a mirror. Since light bends when it enters or exits water, what a salmon sees through this window is functionally larger than the diameter of the window. This is the same light-bending phenomenon as what one sees when plunging a stick into the water. The stick will appear to bend at the point where it enters the water. Therefore, from the angler's perspective a fish will appear both deeper and closer than its actual position.

As a fish approaches the surface in response to a surface fly the diameter of the window decreases proportionally. When it is immediately under the surface the window is very small. A fly on the water outside the circumference of the window will simply appear as indentations in a mirror except for the parts of the fly that penetrate the water surface.

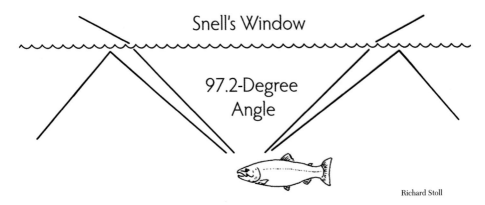

Richard Stoll

The above depicts both refraction at the edges of Snell's window and reflection on the undersurface of the water outside of the window.

When stripping a surface fly like a Miyawaki Popper ripples will distort the surface outside of the window. It follows then that color and detail may often be a moot point in surface-fly design. Conversely, the ripples a fly makes when stripped may become an important factor in eliciting a response.

Do Salmon See Color?

Fish eyes allow for some degree of color discrimination but not nearly as much as human eyes. Research has shown that salmon have a range of color vision that extends further into the blue to ultraviolet ranges than human eyes. Salmon have relatively poor vision for higher-spectrum colors such as reds, oranges and yellows. Likewise, salmon show a preference for blue under most background and light conditions. Further, salmon are able to differentiate between subtle differences of shades of blue, but not for other colors. (Appendix II).

In any event, a full range of color vision is not possible below approximately ten feet in depth in gin-clear water, and as shallow as one to two feet in turbid or cloudy water. Colors such as reds, then oranges and yellows filter out progressively with depth. Greens and then blues saturate deeper water landscapes. Below sixty feet at best and possibly far shallower depending on water conditions, the blue side of the spectrum dominates. If fly color is important it follows then consideration should be given to tying flies with materials in the blue to ultraviolet range, all other factors considered.

Salmonid vision changes significantly when they move from saltwater into rivers. The retina in their eyes changes to see longer wavelength colors such as yellow, orange and red (Kageyama, 1999). They also become more sensitive to UV light. These are likely important adaptations for sexual recognition during spawning, among other factors. Salmon must also adapt to the brighter light regimes in streams and rivers because their pupils do not contract in bright light conditions as human pupils do.

This makes biological sense. Salmon are adapted to see best in the blue to ultraviolet color ranges of the deeper water landscapes where they often feed.

In shallower waters where longer wavelength colors are much more intense, these colors will diminish in intensity with increasing horizontal distance from the fish (Figure 1-8). This means that when flies tied with red, pink, and orange are away in any direction, they will increasingly appear colorless, gray, or black. For example, reds will turn to gray, then black with distance and/or depth. Depending on ambient underwater light intensity, these neutral colors may provide an excellent silhouette against a water backdrop and may become quite visible to the fish.

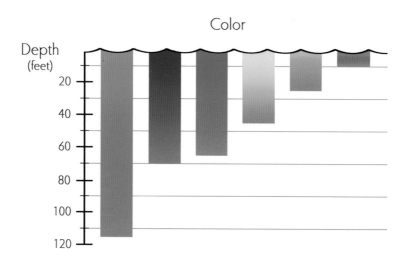

Figure 1-8. When light enters the water its intensity decreases and the colors it imparts to objects starts to immediately decrease beginning with longer wavelengths; red, orange, yellow, with red fastest. The more turbid the water with suspended and dissolved materials the faster these colors diminish.

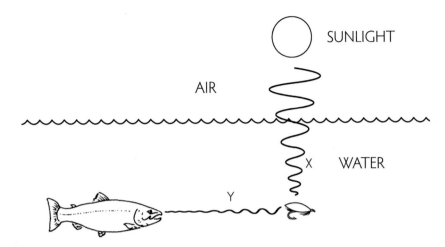

From a fish's visual perspective, color also attenuates horizontally with total distance it travels through the water (x distance + y distance).

Both juveniles and salmon close to sexual maturity have been shown to have increased sensitivity to ultraviolet light. Salmon that specialize in feeding on plankton, like Sockeye and Pinks also have a higher sensitivity to ultraviolet light throughout much of their adult lives. This may be because many crustaceans and other plankton species exhibit ultraviolet hues in their coloration.

In some cases, color is simply not an issue. Salmon most easily observe the fly from below. This is often the case when flies are fished shallow or on the surface. Where the fly is between the fish and the surface it is silhouetted against the sky. Where this happens fish will most often see a gray or black silhouette rather than bright colors.

The upshot is that salmon often do not see red if at all under some conditions. This may be true even in the clearest of waters. When salmon do see some red, red diminishes very quickly with increasing water depth eventually turning to gray, then black. The same is true to a diminishing degree with other longer wavelength colors such as shades of pink, orange, and yellow.

As evening dark approaches salmon vision changes and loses its ability to see color in favor of grays and blacks. Color vision returns in daylight, but possibly not at depths where full-color spectrums do not exist. The question then arises as to why some red-colored flies and lures can be so effective in the evening and at depth. The answer may be that darker colors like blues and black have a much more distinct silhouette and are therefore much more visible.

Nevertheless, we fly anglers love our intricately tied and colorful flies. We will continue to tie and fish these flies for the aesthetics, that is how we feel, what we imagine fish may see, or simply to peak our angling imaginations.

How Do Silhouette, Contrast, and Color Interact in Salmon Feeding Behavior?

Even though salmon have limited perception for brighter colors, at times these colors appear to be significant in lure design. For example, red-colored lures are often preferred by both anglers and fish at depths where the color red is virtually nonexistent. Likewise, at times pastel hues like pink and orange, or white are sometimes preferred by both anglers and fish at shallower depths.

On the other hand, baitfish and other prey species are in shades and colors that are least visible to predators. These are colors that closely match the surrounding environment. They do not stand out against the aquatic background which renders them less visible to predators. It is not uncommon for deep-water fish to be bright colored in air. For example, yellow-eye rockfish and canary rockfish are predominantly orange and yellow in air. However, at depths where these colors do not exist, the lack of contrast rendered by yellow and orange cause these fish to be much less visible to both predators and prey in their deep-water environments.

Red is another issue. Red becomes increasingly dark, tending toward black with depth. In black-and-white movies directors and set designers used red to provide greater contrast. Colors of similar shades reduced contrast therefore object definition. This is the case with red in deeper aquatic environments. Although the color red is muted even in relatively shallow depths, it does provide silhouette and contrast that is more visible to fish.

What is the Importance of Fluorescence and Flash in Salmon Feeding Behavior?

As many anglers are intuitively aware fluorescence is often an important consideration in the design of salmon flies. Some of the most effective salmon flies are tied with fluorescent materials. Fluorescence captures light of one wavelength and then emits light most often of a longer and more visible wavelength. This is the reason that high light-emitting colors like fluorescent chartreuse seem so effective in deeper water. Non-fluorescent chartreuse would otherwise be substantially muted in color. As such, fluorescence makes a fly stand out only when there is adequate light for fluorescence to happen. It follows then, that fluorescent flies are much more visible in deeper water environments where adequate light conditions exist to allow fluorescence to happen.

The top picture was taken in bright sunlight of materials in the same char-treuse color. All were labeled as fluorescent and indeed appear to be so. The bottom picture was taken under blue light to simulate the higher energy colors that dominate underwater seascapes. Only two of the materials were fluorescent. However, they had lost most of their chartreuse color, as would be expected in a deeper water environment. This demonstrates the impor-tance that materials used in the construction of fluorescent flies are actually fluorescent. This can be easily checked using an inexpensive blue or black light carried in most hardware stores.

Flash is akin to fluorescence in that flashy materials give off light, but only by reflection of existing ambient light. The flashing silver sides of both fleeing prey and feeding salmon is a phenomenon that often incites salmon to aggressively feed.

Does The Lateral Line Have A Function In Salmon Feeding Behavior?

Lateral lines run along the center of each side of a fish body. Lateral lines are unique in that they combine the functional aspects of touch, hearing and sight. Fish acutely sense water movements, micro currents, waves, and near-field very low frequency sounds with their lateral lines. Lateral lines can detect minute and overlapping pressure waves caused by water movements from multiple sources, all at the same time. Because, like eyes, lateral lines are on each side of a fish, fish can often tell the direction from which these waves are coming. This is an important feeding adaptation, especially in low-light conditions.

Salmon appear to sense waves emanating from different surface and underwater sources as distinctly different. These distinct waves may include those made by swimming baitfish, or schools of baitfish as the case may be. Salmon appear to be able to sense prey fish movements acutely and directionally to a highly sophisticated degree. Therefore, as a feeding response mechanism, the lateral line may often be more important than sight! How this may impact the construction of salmon flies is a fly-tying issue that should be taken into consideration as has been the case with some of the fly patterns described in this book.

What Effect Does Smell Have On Salmon Feeding Behavior?

A number of species of fish are known to have a very highly developed sense of smell. Fish nasal organs called olfactory lobes appear to be able to detect some classes of chemical compounds into the parts-per-billion, or lower. It has been experimentally demonstrated that when salmon get close to their spawning streams that they appear to discern the minute and unique chemical characteristics of that stream.

Likewise, many fish, including salmon appear to respond to the smell of prey. This lends logic to the reason many terminal-tackle salmon fishers prefer real bait such as herring as opposed to artificial. Bass fishermen often apply smell potions on their baits. Likewise, in some saltwater situations, spraying artificial lures with WD-40 seems to increase their effectiveness for some highly migratory ocean fish species. While adding smell may be effective in certain situations, such enhancements are rare among fly-anglers.

It has also been demonstrated that a chemical in oils found in human skin, the amino acid L-serine, may be repulsive to some fish species. So, it makes good sense to minimize skin contact with the water while fishing. This may also be true of other substances like sunscreens, insect repellents, and possibly petroleum products like oil and gasoline.

How Do Salmon Respond To Sound?

Sound is a very significant factor in aquatic environments. The underwater soundscape is diverse, sometimes intense, and can be much more pervasive than in air. This is especially true in inner sounds and bays where there is a lot of boat traffic, pile driving, sonar, and the like. But sound does not have direct significance for the fly-angler under most circumstances except to note that sound does not efficiently travel across the air-water interface. Therefore salmon often will not hear sounds created in the air above the water. Conversely, salmon are acutely sensitive to low-frequency underwater sounds. Noises that travel through the bottom of a boat, like pounding or dropping an anchor, can be heard very well under water and can affect salmon behavior. Pervasive "sound pollution" may also have a significant impact on salmon survival (Appendix II).

When and Under What Conditions Do Salmon Most Actively Feed?

Salmon-tagging studies in Puget Sound and elsewhere have shown that peak salmon feeding periods are variable occurring both during the day and night, but most often during early morning and evening hours when ambient light levels are low. This, and the fact that salmon often feed at depths in excess of sixty feet where light is limited, means that salmon can perceive prey in darker conditions when most colors are not visible.

It should also be noted that salmon eyes are relatively large as compared to body size. Likewise their large pupils allow for a high level of light-gathering capability. Salmon are adapted to feeding and avoiding predators during low-light conditions as is the case at night and at depth. It therefore makes sense that they can see well-designed flies under relatively dark conditions. Well-designed includes characteristics such as darker colors and hues in the blue to ultraviolet ranges. In any case, dark colors create a more distinct silhouette against the sky or a water background.

Why Do Returning Salmon Jump?

A discussion on why salmon jump is useful and informative. In the case of terminal pre-spawning salmon in estuaries and river mouths, an individual jumping can indicate the location of a school below.

Why salmon jump has been a subject of discussion amongst salmon anglers ever since salmon angling became a popular sport, maybe even before. One old-anglers-tale purports that they do this to loosen their eggs. But this does not explain why male fish do at least half of the jumping. Another angler theory alleges that salmon are readying themselves to negotiate obstacles and water falls in their upstream journey. But they need to conserve energy, not use it, to prepare for the journey upstream. Both theories seem rather far-fetched.

As fisheries science would postulate, salmon find their way around the Pacific Ocean by some sort of gravitational or celestial navigation system that we know little about. When salmon are close to their spawning streams it is known that their navigation changes to a more targeted mode; that is the unique smell of their particular spawning stream.

Fresh water is less dense than salt water. Given little mixing occurs from wind or waves, fresh water will float on salt water. As a result, fresh stream water running into a saltwater estuary acts like gasoline on water. Fresh water spreads out into a very thin layer across the surface of the saltwater until such time as wind and waves mix it into the upper layers of the saltwater.

Therefore, if smell is the mechanism for recognizing a stream, salmon cannot smell their home stream very well if they are swimming at depth. So, it appears that salmon jump through the surface in an attempt to "smell" their home stream. The next time you watch a salmon jump, observe the way it jumps. Most often salmon appear to jump in such a way as to scoop water in their nares. Nare is the term used for the two nasal orifices. The nares are located on each side of the head in front of the eyes. Most observant salmon anglers will have noticed that salmon nare appear to greatly enlarge as they get closer to their spawning streams. When salmon jump they scoop surface water into these enlarged nasal openings. Chum salmon are most obvious in this behavior. They will often flop on their sides and paddle themselves along the surface scooping up surface water into their nares.

The practical application to this is where one salmon jumps, there are likely more salmon below. I personally have had great success casting to jumping salmon, especially in estuaries and bays near their natal rivers.

Salmon often reveal themselves when they jump.
This salmon was taken by Bill Drewry, owner of Peninsula
Outfitters Fly Shop in Poulsbo, Washington.

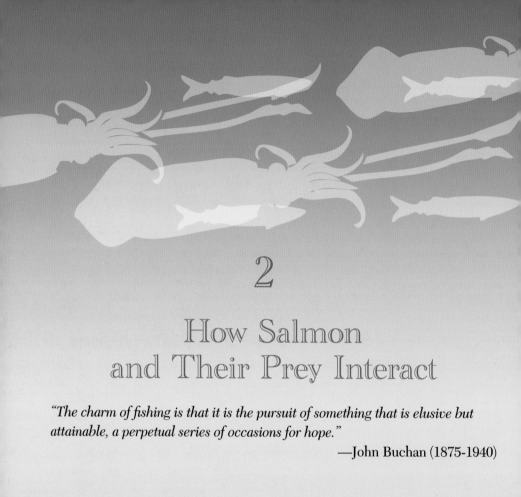

2

How Salmon
and Their Prey Interact

"The charm of fishing is that it is the pursuit of something that is elusive but attainable, a perpetual series of occasions for hope."

—John Buchan (1875-1940)

What Do Salmon Eat?

Salmon feed on a variety of fish and invertebrates ranging from zooplankton and squid to baitfish depending on salmon species, life stage and location. By and large baitfish imitations are the most important to inshore saltwater fly-anglers in pursuit of larger salmon with notable exceptions. Smaller juvenile Coho and juvenile Chinook often feed on zooplankton, sometimes exclusively.

The four most important baitfish are herring, candlefish, surf smelt, and northern anchovy (Appendix III). Of these four, candlefish then herring are the most important to inshore saltwater fly anglers. These are the most prevalent prey species during the summer to fall salmon in-migrations. Surf smelt and northern anchovy are the least important. Smelt are available a very short period during the season. Northern Anchovy are photophobic to some degree (adverse to light) and dive far deeper than salmon are able to forage during fishable daylight hours. This being understood, when foraging in inshore waters, salmon will opportunistically target almost any small fish and many invertebrates. After all, salmon make a living by eating as much as possible.

Salmon are both opportunistic and curious. A salmon's mouth is the functional equivalent of hands. They will pick up, drop, and sometimes consume debris and varieties of marine biota. These also include the often very abundant free-swimming megalops larvae of the Dungeness crab and a myriad of small shrimp-like animals. Salmon sometimes will also pick up flies that do not necessarily resemble what they have been eating. Remember that 'big red fly' you had that worked so well one day and then never worked again?

Wherever possible larger feeding salmon will focus on concentrations of baitfish. From a biological perspective it is energetically necessary to do so. Larger salmon do not actively pursue small prey in inshore waters unless they are in very dense concentrations. An exception may be in shallow areas with a lot of bottom structure and eel grass and seaweed. These areas provide rich habitat for a host of potential food organisms. I have seen large Coho salmon rooting around eelgrass beds in as shallow as two feet of water.

Where there is prey in adequate concentrations there is a good possibility salmon may be present. These include more productive situations such as in and around baitfish schools and in near-shore areas where there is structure that affords food and protection for a variety of prey species.

Smaller juvenile Coho and Chinook to some lesser degree opportunistically feed on zooplankton as the major part of their diets. Juvenile Chinook and Coho eyes are more sensitive to the ultraviolet colors that many of these invertebrates exhibit. Chum, Pinks and Sockeye largely subsist on plankton and larger invertebrates, such as squid, a substantial part of their life spans. Chums, Pinks, and Sockeye also appear to be more sensitive to ultraviolet hues than Coho and Chinook. This is likely a feeding adaptation that allows them to visually locate prey in deeper ocean waters.

Of particular importance to pre-migration juvenile Coho salmon are the free-swimming megalops larvae of the Dungeness crab. Megalops larvae occur in very large numbers in northern salt waters from the spring to fall. They range in the water column from the surface to 75 feet deep, mostly depending on time of day. Fisheries biologists have postulated that in some years juvenile Coho can feed so heavily on these larvae as to affect adult crab populations in future years. It has also been stated by whale biologists that during some years megalops larvae are so dense that they may be important to gray whale feeding. Megalops larvae are about a quarter the diameter of a dime. They are within the very size and UV or fluorescent color ranges that imitations like green and pink Wheenies make great imitations for targeting juvenile salmon.

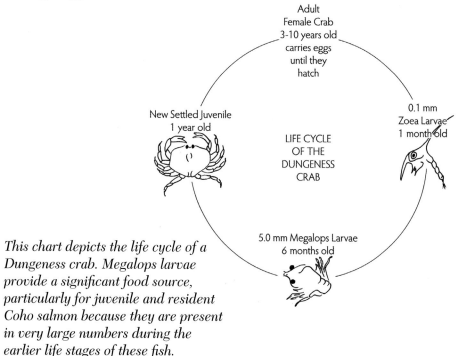

This chart depicts the life cycle of a Dungeness crab. Megalops larvae provide a significant food source, particularly for juvenile and resident Coho salmon because they are present in very large numbers during the earlier life stages of these fish.

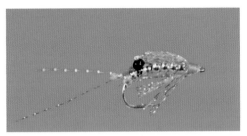

A Megalops larvae and its imitation, the Green Wheenie.

How Do Salmon Behave Around Bait Schools?

The behaviors of salmon and baitfish revolve around one another. Likewise, their interactions make baitfish available to many other predators, including fish, birds and seals. Chinook salmon, and to some lesser but significant degree Coho salmon, are the shepherds of the sea. They often herd baitfish into dense schools. They post sentinels around the sides and bottoms of these schools. Those who have spent a lot of time observing baitfish on fish-finders have seen dense schools of baitfish with a few large fish at various points around these schools.

In shallow water, feeding salmon are rarely found above schools of baitfish. They feed from the sides and below. This is partially a consequence of their field of vision as discussed in Chapter One. Conversely, in deep water where perception may often be more through the lateral line than sight, salmon often locate themselves above baitfish. This is most often the case when schools of baitfish are on or near the bottom.

Most often salmon do not pick off healthy individuals from the edges of the schools, nor are they predisposed to chasing individual prey located in a school. Doing so would cause them to expend a great deal of energy with very little to show for the effort. Healthy baitfish are quick and very difficult to catch.

When a baitfish school is some distance up in the water column, typical salmon strategy appears to be one or two salmon charging directly through the school. In the process baitfish are injured. Salmon are then able to forage on injured baitfish without expending a great deal of energy.

During daylight hours larger Chinook salmon move deeper in the water column where light is limited. Large Chinook salmon are most often

Sills are underwater dams. In fjords they are most often a glacier's terminal moraine. In many cases they are also caused by extreme tidal currents in front of bays bounded by points or promontories.

found at or near the bottom beneath schools of baitfish, even if these schools are close to the surface. They wait for the injured prey to fall to them. This phenomenon is also apparent in the generally non-aggressive way that large Chinook salmon take a mooched herring. This may also account in part as to why some salmon get so much larger than others. One might compare this to pot-bellied TV sports enthusiasts. We stuff ourselves watching the game doing very little physical work in the process.

When baitfish schools are herded next to the bottom they funnel upwards in a maneuver turned in the direction of the current. On a fish-finder this configuration looks like an upside down tornado. Salmon use the bottom to their advantage. While they shepherd the sides of the school, panicked baitfish injure themselves on the bottom.

When pursued by salmon from below, herring can often be seen as roiling masses of fish in a constant state of motion. Dense schools constantly change shape and form like a giant amoeba. They will sometimes move at speeds in excess of four to five knots, especially when moving with a running tide. I have observed large schools of herring bulge as high as several inches above the surface of the water. On one occasion I observed a bald eagle and several seagulls land on top of one of these bulging schools and gorge themselves so much that they had difficulty taking off.

Under the right conditions salmon will push schools of baitfish right up against shores, making the salmon accessible to beach anglers. Most commonly these are areas where sand bars and spits have been naturally formed by tides and currents. There is usually a bar or sill associated with one or both sides of these promontories. In water usually less than 140 feet in depth salmon and prey will spatially disperse along sills and drop-offs. When the tidal currents flow along these sills toward shoreline bars and spits the inevitable happens, baitfish are pushed up onto the shoreline. Salmon aggressively follow these baitfish into the shallows, often pushing them up into mere inches of water. These salmon are very vulnerable to flies like the Mylar Baitfish that imitates injured or fleeing baitfish.

Effects of Tides on Salmon Feeding

Understanding the effects of tides is crucial to deciding when and where to fish for salmon in salt water. Tides are caused by the gravitational pull of the sun and moon either together or separately. During the times of the year when the moon and sun are in alignment, the combined gravitational pull from both causes very high tides which are followed by very low tides. These extreme tides are called spring tides. Spring tides are accompanied by higher velocity tidal currents. When the sun and moon are separated by 90 degrees as viewed from the earth the tidal exchanges are mild. These mild tides are called neap tides. Neap tides have much lower velocity currents.

Current velocities have a significant effect on salmon feeding behavior. Because of their shape and form, salmon appear to function best when facing into currents with velocities of approximately one-half to two knots.

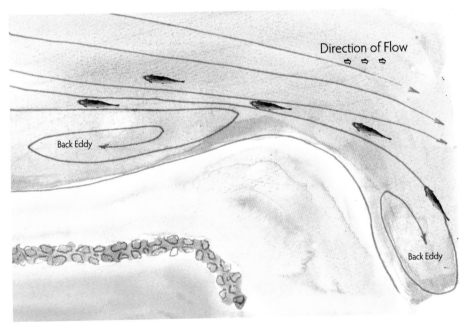

An incoming tidal set up at Point no Point. Strong back-eddy currents containing divergent currents are confusing to salmon. Salmon prefer to swim into currents due to their torpedo shape and to keep water flowing across their gills and stay out of severe back eddies. Salmon tend to congregate next to eddies where bait is more highly concentrated.

At these velocities salmon can move forward into the current with minimal use of fins almost as fast as they are being pushed back. This allows for substantial energy conservation. Energy conservation is of key importance for salmon survival. Salmon need to put as much of their bodily energy resources as possible into the generation of eggs and sperm. They also need to ensure optimal size and strength for navigating their home river. Lastly, they will need to be fit to compete with other salmon during the spawning process.

During periods of high-velocity tidal currents salmon will actively seek locations where there are more ideal water velocities. These locations are often near the bottom, next to eddies, or next to obstructions. Salmon also avoid actively swimming downstream in faster currents. This is because they will have to move substantially faster than the current to ensure adequate water across their gills. When deciding where, when, and how to fish salmon from beaches, both tidal velocity and current direction should be taken into account.

The above discussions lead to an important conclusion. When baitfish are present, salmon will push them onto beaches and along spits, drop-offs, and sills. If tidal velocity is not in excess of approximately 2.0 knots, salmon will be in hot pursuit and most available to inshore fly anglers.

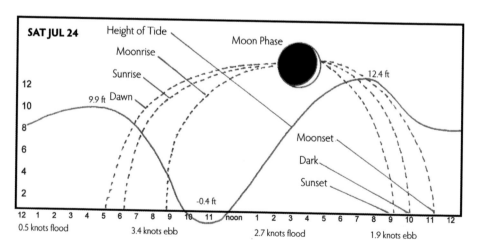

Easy to read and comprehensive tide tables are one of the most important saltwater fly-angling tools. Tables should clearly show tide stages, velocities, and time of day. One of the best commercially available tide books is Tidelog by Pacific Publishers, LLC.

Other Environmental Factors that Affect When and How Salmon Feed

Light Intensity

The intensity of ambient light is related to time of day, time of year, and the density of cloud cover. Different salmon species react to light in different ways. For example, with the exception of juveniles Chinook salmon avoid bright light. When sunlight is on the water, larger Chinook usually migrate to depths between sixty and one hundred forty feet. During very low light conditions and at night Chinook salmon will often move into very shallow water to feed. Therefore, the best time to fish for larger Chinook salmon in shallow water is just before sunrise or just after sunset. This is when there is still enough light for the angler to see.

Coho salmon are much more light tolerant. In open water Coho often prefer water less than thirty feet deep and can often be found near the surface. Coho will concentrate around tide rip accumulations of foam, flotsam, and jetsam at the surface. Locating Coho in open water is often a matter of locating surface rips and debris, or by chasing feeding flocks of feeding sea birds.

Paul Stoll

Where there are birds feeding on the surface, salmon are often not far below.

In-migrating pink salmon are often found in shallow waters under relatively bright light conditions. They can often be dispersed amongst Coho salmon.

There is common angler wisdom that when there is a full moon salmon can see to feed at night. Consequently the bite goes off during the day. I do not find this to always be the case. Given the opportunity and right conditions salmon will opportunistically feed when there are opportunities to feed. This is regardless of night light conditions, either near the surface or at depth.

Changing Barometer

Anglers have long known that changing weather affects fish behavior. I can't count the number of times I have heard anglers say that when the barometer falls, the fish bite goes off. In Puget Sound many anglers believe when there is a north wind the bite will be poor. A north wind in the Puget Sound is usually associated with a falling barometer. A falling barometer represents a drop in atmospheric pressure.

Considering that fish experience significant pressure changes with relatively small changes in water depth, the comparatively very small barometric pressure changes would seem to be insignificant. It therefore appears very unlikely that changes in barometric pressure in and of itself would affect fish feeding. It is more likely is that weather conditions coincident with pressure changes can affect the bite. These conditions might include wind, turbidity caused by wind and rain, wind generated waves, and a general reduction in underwater visibility.

Turbidity

Turbidity is a scattering of light by particles in the water including silt, sand, or dense plankton. Turbidity decreases light penetration into the water column. Near-shore turbidity is usually caused by wind and waves stirring up the bottom. Wind and waves are often associated with changing barometric pressure. Excessive turbidity is abrasive to salmon gills and eyes and reduces their ability to see. This, in turn affects the ability of salmon to find prey. They will seek deeper and often clearer water.

Temperature

Optimal temperatures for salmon are approximately forty-five to fifty-five degrees depending on a number of variables. In colder water salmon metabolism slows. Conversely, salmon become more active and aggressive when the temperature rises into the mid-fifties. Salmon become physically stressed when the temperature is above sixty and are reticent to feed. Temperatures in the 70s can be lethal. Inshore salt waters generally stay within optimal temperature ranges. However, in shallow areas excessive sunlight reflecting off a light-colored sand bottom can cause temperatures to rise high enough to affect salmon behavior. This can affect the quality of fishing in the often shallow estuaries where fish stage before running up a stream to spawn.

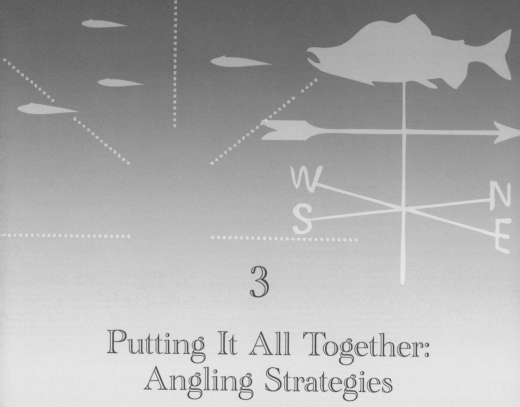

3

Putting It All Together: Angling Strategies

"Game fish are too valuable to be caught only once."

—Lee Wulff, 1939

Important considerations in planning a fishing trip include tides and currents, weather, light conditions, and turbidity. Optimal fishing conditions include optimal combinations of most of these factors. For example, Point no Point, a popular angling beach in northern Puget Sound, fishes best on a low to incoming tide with velocities between 0.5 to 2.0 knots. This is an ideal velocity range for salmon to most efficiently feed in. The ideal time of day is when a low-velocity incoming tide just after the low occurs near sunrise or in the late evening. Incoming tides push both salmon and bait off of an underwater sill that extends out about a quarter mile to the northwest back on to the beach. Wind direction should be from the southeast accompanied by a high and steady barometer. Wind velocity should not exceed ten knots. Higher winds will cause excessive turbidity and will make it difficult to cast a fly line.

Ideal fishing conditions vary depending on locality. A beach several miles south of Point no Point is best on either side of an extreme low tide. The difference between Point no Point and this other beach is that Point no Point has a relatively significant drop-off over a sandy beach. The other beach is composed of flats with a very gentle drop-off and dense eelgrass beds. Tidal velocity is greatly reduced over these eel grass flats during the high-velocity tides that make it very difficult to fly-fish at Point no Point. These flats provide a salmon feeding refuge from the higher velocity waters off shore. Salmon come up over the drop-off and forage on bait-fish hiding in and around these eelgrass beds. This creates an ideal situation for wading fly anglers.

The author with a bright Situk estuary Coho, Yakutat, Alaska.

Trip-Planning Strategies

Consult Your Tide Table

Tides are an accessibility issue as well as a factor that affects salmon behavior. It is expedient to learn how salmon respond to tidal flows in different fishing locations. In most locations either side of a low tide is optimal, especially on beaches where seaweed, eel grass and bottom structure harbors prey. In other locations higher tides are optimal. These may include estuaries that become deep enough during higher tides for salmon to move close to shore where they become more accessible to wading anglers. On the other hand if tides are too extreme they can exceed optimal velocities for salmon feeding.

Know the Timing of Local Salmon Runs

Most mature salmon in-migrate mid-summer to late fall. If one is targeting Coho or Pink salmon, consult local resources to find locations where these fish are known to occur within any particular time frame. These time frames can vary within geographic areas and even vary from year to year by several weeks. One thing is certain. Returning salmon will eventually end up near or in the estuaries of their spawning rivers.

While there are excellent run-timing charts such as those in *Fly-Fishing for Pacific Salmon II* (Johnson, et. al. 2008), these charts only give very general information as to what species can be found in a geographical area at any time of the year. Therefore, run-timing charts are generally of limited value for any particular beach, estuary, stream, or watershed.

It is expedient to fish where the fish are most likely to occur. When planning a fishing trip to a location one is not familiar with it is a good idea to consult local fishing shops or other knowledgeable persons. Fishing regulations can also change from what is published during the course of a season to include such things as emergency closures, another reason to consult a local fly fishing shop.

Check the Weather Forecast

Wind forecasts should be of special interest. Windy conditions can create waves and turbid water which will put down near shore salmon feeding. Depending on wind direction, windy conditions can also make casting very difficult.

Consult the State Fishing Regulations

First check the state annual fishing regulations pamphlet. But also be aware that for any given location there may be special in-season rules that may not show up in the regulations pamphlet. Salmon quotas may change depending on a lower actual run size than projected run sizes. There may also be special regulations for catch and release and barbless hooks. For in-season updates it is best to also check the web site of the state fisheries agency.

On-the-Water Strategies

Following are strategies for catching all five species of salmon; Coho, Chinook, Chum, Pink, Sockeye. Of these, Coho are the most ideally suited salmon for fly-angling. Therefore, more space is devoted to Coho than other salmon species.

Mark Salo

The author releasing a bright tidewater-caught Coho salmon.

Bears are not uncommon around Alaska rivers during salmon runs.

Coho Salmon

Fly-anglers can effectively target and catch Coho in a variety of situations. Among these are beaches, estuaries, open water, and as juvenile residents.

Beaches, Points and Promontories

During annual in-migrations from central California to southern Alaska, Coho can often be found actively feeding in shallow waters near beaches, promontories, and points of land. Under certain tidal and low-light conditions Coho will make feeding forays from deeper water into water as shallow as two feet. The quality of beach fishing depends on factors discussed in previous chapters including the near-shore density of prey species. This can vary greatly from day to day. Further,

When baitfish are present Coho salmon will actively forage in water as shallow as two feet. In these situations it is often expedient to make casts that parallel the shore line.

each individual location has special characteristics that can affect fishing. These can be learned from spending a lot of time on the water, consulting other fly anglers, or consulting experts in local fly fishing shops.

Coho generally avoid the circular flows of back eddies that are often coincident with points and promontories during faster running tides. The multi-directional water flows that occur in eddies confuse many fish species. Fish are designed to swim into the current. This ensures for adequate oxygenation of their gills. Coho prefer swimming into laminar flows including those in adjacent to rips and eddies. These areas concentrate prey species to create more optimal feeding conditions.

Under these conditions it is expedient to use a baitfish imitation on a floating, sink-tip, or intermediate sinking line. I find a floating line easier for line management. Underwater currents often push sinking fly lines in odd and divergent directions making it difficult to control the fly. Ideal flies under these conditions include the Coho Special and Miyawaki Popper. Alternatively, Clousers, Angel-Hair Candlefish or Mylar Baitfish can be very effective.

When searching open water along the Straights of San Juan de Fuca, Puget Sound, and other inland beach areas, salmon will sometimes briefly congregate where there is freshwater inflow even though the water is not emanating from their spawning stream.

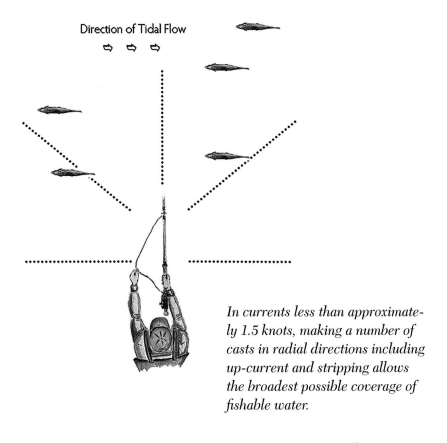

Direction of Tidal Flow

In currents less than approximately 1.5 knots, making a number of casts in radial directions including up-current and stripping allows the broadest possible coverage of fishable water.

Vary stripping speed from slow to somewhat erratic with a slight pause between strips. Coho will often pick up the fly on the pause. With surface flies like the Miyawaki Popper simply creating an even v-wake on the surface is often enough to incite an aggressive response. It is common for Coho to visibly bulge behind a surface waking fly, dorsal fin out of the water. When this happens, speeding up the strip or changing direction of the fly by moving the rod tip will often cause the fish to take. When the take does come it is important not to immediately set the hook. This will often pull the fly away from the fish. Simply wait until you feel pressure on the line then raise the rod.

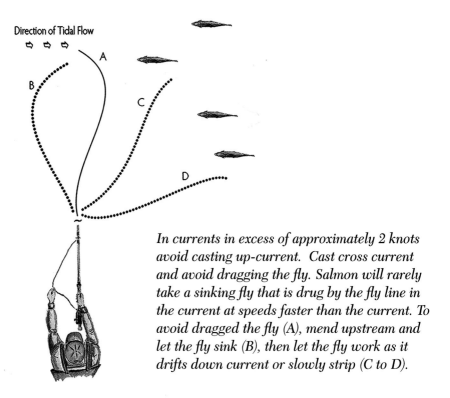

Direction of Tidal Flow

A

B

C

D

In currents in excess of approximately 2 knots avoid casting up-current. Cast cross current and avoid dragging the fly. Salmon will rarely take a sinking fly that is drug by the fly line in the current at speeds faster than the current. To avoid dragged the fly (A), mend upstream and let the fly sink (B), then let the fly work as it drifts down current or slowly strip (C to D).

Estuaries, Bays, and Terminal Inlets

When Coho salmon arrive in the estuaries of their natal streams they most often stage in schools. These schools will meander around estuaries and adjacent saltwaters until such time that river flow and tide conditions allow them to run up stream. In these situations the concentrations of salmon presents a fine angling opportunity. Individual fish most often spurn all types of offerings including flies that represent prey. This can be very frustrating to anglers. While these terminal Coho have stopped feeding for nutritional purposes they sometimes can be enticed take offerings as a conditioned response or as aggression.

Some years ago I was visiting a friend's home in Homer, Alaska. At that time John Martin was Manager of the Alaska Maritime Wildlife Refuge. John was a very knowledgeable biologist as well as a fine fly angler. That particular visit John took me on a drive to see large schools of Coho located off the spit in Kachemak Bay. I was amazed to see hundreds of fish milling along the shoreline. I was ready to string-up my fly rod. But John warned

The author blind-casting open areas between eelgrass beds.
Feeding salmon will often make foraging runs between and
next to eelgrass beds in search of prey.

me that these fish were nearly impossible to take. He assured me he had
tried many times. Likewise, a dozen or so terminal-tackle anglers lining the
shoreline were having very little luck except for the occasional snagged fish.
Nevertheless, at my urging John agreed to launch his boat the next day so
we could have a reasonable shot at these fish while avoiding the crowds.

I introduced John to flies and techniques first explored by a former fly
fishing shop partner, Bob Searle. These techniques had been developed
for targeting large schools of terminal Coho in Miller Bay, a Puget Sound
estuary. To John's amazement, as well as the amazement of a number of
shoreline anglers, we hooked one fish after another until our arms were
near exhaustion.

We were using a size-8 Fluorescent Green Wheenie. This fly is most
effective on a floating line stripped very slowly with long pauses in between
strips. Terminal Coho are often attracted to very small fluorescent flies when
the sun is on the water.

An interesting but substantially unexplainable phenomenon is that terminal Coho can turn the bite off and on, very much like switching a light
switch on and off. For a period of time it seems every fish in the area will
take, regardless of whether they are in a school or not. Then the bite can
stop. It has been postulated that fish in the same vicinity communicate by
release of minute amounts of pheromones or some other organic com-
pound into the water.

Male Coho salmon taken off a Puget Sound beach. A hooked nose, termed a kype, is distinctly visible. This is an indication that this fish was in the last stages of developing male spawning features.

It is not generally productive to blind-cast for terminal Coho. It is more productive to lead cast a moving school. In shallower water fish are visible by the wakes they make. Otherwise, target jumping fish. Where one fish jumps, there are usually more fish beneath.

Open Water

While open-water techniques requiring a sea-worthy boat are not the primary focus of this book, it seems useful to mention some aspects of open-water Coho fisheries. Coho salmon can be taken in open water in a number of locations along the coasts of Washington, British Columbia, and Alaska when in large schools are near the ocean surface. One favorite spot is several miles out of Neah Bay, the northwestern point of Washington State at the entrance to the Straights of San Juan de Fuca. In late summer fly anglers are often seen fishing in the general vicinity of a small mid-channel rock outcropping in the center of the channel called Duncan Rocks. In past years it was not unusual to hook numbers of fish in the double digits. Runs have declined in recent years.

Coho salmon have an affinity for feeding around tidal current lines and accumulations of flotsam and jetsam. These areas concentrate baitfish as well as provide protection from bright sun and predators. Once fish are

*Mark Salo and Jim Russell casting to terminal Coho in
Miller Bay, an estuary in central Puget Sound.*

located it is simply a matter of casting a baitfish imitation, letting it sink,
then stripping it back. Intermediate or fast-sinking fly lines are ideal. Open-
water Coho will often preferentially take very-fast-stripped flies, but not
always. An effective fast-tripping technique is to hold the fly rod under an
arm and quickly strip with both hands.

Open-water Coho can also be located by observing the presence of feeding birds or panicked surface schools of baitfish. When birds are diving from
above there is a good possibility of salmon below.

Resident Coho

Small resident Coho provide a great off-season fly fishery in Puget Sound
as well as in parts of British Columbia. The Washington State Department
of Fish and Wildlife created a resident Coho enhancement program
expressly for this purpose. This program is based on the fact that late-
released Coho fry tend not to migrate to sea. These resident fish can often
be found much of the winter in fast-moving schools in the southern part
of the Puget Sound. It is best to chase visibly feeding schools with a boat,
but they can also be taken from beaches. Generally speaking, if you can
get a small fly to these schools, the fish will aggressively compete for the
fly. Particularly effective dry flies are Pete's Popper and the Mini Gurgler.

Ted Teather with a nice brace of southeast Alaska Coho. Ruffit Lodge on Prince of Wales Island is in the background.

These should be stripped across the surface just fast enough to make a distinct V-wake. Great wet flies are UV pink or Fluorescent Green Wheenies.

During November, eight-to twelve-inch resident Puget Sound Coho start to migrate north. They stop somewhere around Point no Point in the October time frame. At that time they can run in the two-to-five pound range. Many are coming into sexual maturity. I have personally taken October fish in full spawning condition off Point no Point nowhere near a stream. It is likely these are "lost" fish with no natal stream to target. If this is the case, they will likely die in salt water.

Chinook Salmon

By nature, Chinook salmon are a deeper running salmon. They are generally not as accessible to fly anglers as Coho, Chum and Pinks, except in their juvenile stages. The few larger Chinook taken off beaches are usually coincidentally hooked while fishing for Coho or Pinks late evenings or early mornings. But there are notable exceptions.

Beaches, Points or Promontories

Almost all larger Chinook salmon taken by fly anglers off beaches points and promontories are incidental catches. Most are caught at lower tides. During early morning or late-evening hours Chinook will often forage near beaches and sometimes in very shallow waters. Several times while wading beaches late evenings I have seen small schools of Chinook chasing bait into as shallow as three or four feet of water. One late evening, while wading near-shore shallows, a school of four or five large fish came so close to me I could have impaled one with the tip of my fly rod.

Unlike the Coho inclination to pick up a fly on the pause between strips, Chinook seem more inclined to pick up a fly on a slow steady strip. Deeper-swimming flies such as the Alien, fluorescent or UV Clousers, or heavy epoxy headed flies on a sink-tip or sinking line are more effective than flies fished close to the surface.

Estuaries, Bays, and Terminal Inlets

Chinook salmon can sometimes be taken on a fly when they are staging to run into an estuary or river mouth. The Chinook salmon in below was caught from a school of staging fish in Kachemak Bay in Homer, Alaska using a fluorescent chartreuse Clouser. These fish were in water several feet deep preparing to run into what is locally termed the 'Spit Hole', a juvenile salmon rearing pond located on Homer spit.

The author with a Kachemak Bay Chinook.

Chinook salmon are also occasionally taken on a fly near Juneau in the Gastineau Channel between Douglas Island and the mainland during their May to June runs. Most have been taken with deep-sinking lines. On one instance I hooked a large Chinook off Douglas Island on a low tide while casting a fly from a popular rocky fishing promontory. I lost the fish to a waiting sea lion, not an all-that-uncommon occurrence.

John Martin with a hefty Chinook salmon caught in mild surf at the mouth of the Anchor River, Cook Inlet, Alaska.

Open Water

Taking Chinook in open water is a tough prospect that requires a boat suitable for the purpose, skills at locating fish, patience, and a lot of luck. However, a group of British Columbia fly anglers are specialists in taking Chinook targeting bait schools and feeding birds. There is an excellent discussion on open-water fly-fishing techniques in *Saltwater Fly Fishing for Pacific Salmon* by Barry Thornton (Thornton, 1993). Thornton describes in detail methods for locating salmon by observations of bird activity and by following bait schools. He also describes a hunt-drift-cast method that the author has found to be particularly effective for both Coho and Chinook salmon in British Columbia offshore and inland waters.

Resident Chinook

Washington State Department of Fish and Wildlife has operated a program to enhance resident Chinook in Puget Sound for several years. Chinook tend not to migrate to the open ocean when they are held approximately fourteen months in hatcheries. Over the past number of years as many as 2 million yearling Chinook a year have been late-released for the resident blackmouth fishery.

Resident Chinook behave differently than resident Coho. They do not have as much preponderancy to school and can be somewhat more difficult to target. On the other hand, juvenile resident Chinook are a common inciden-

Ted Teather with a Chinook salmon caught off Kitsap Peninsula on an Alien pattern.

tal catch when fishing for sea-run cutthroat or Coho along Puget Sound beaches. These fish most often run 12 to 20 inches in length, well below the Washington State mandated 22-inch minimum size limit.

Since many Chinook runs have been listed under the Endangered Species Act, be sure to check fishing regulations before targeting these fish. Other than seasonal closures, Chinook salmon rules in Puget Sound require a barbless hook and a minimum length of 22 inches.

Chum Salmon

Estuaries, Bays, and Terminal Inlets

My first attempts at taking Chum salmon on a fly was sometime in the early 1970's. I followed rumors that fellow fly anglers were catching large fish from float tubes at the mouth of Finch Creek adjacent to the Hoodsport salmon hatchery in southern Hood Canal. As it turned out, at lower tides it was possible to simply wade out in front of the hatchery and make short casts with a floating line. This fishery soon became so popular that one fly fishing guide leased the empty lot next to the hatchery for exclusive access. This essentially

Male Chum salmon will often show spawning colors well before entering fresh water.

precluded one of the good accesses to many unhappy fly anglers.

Fly-angling for mature Chum salmon has become exceedingly popular in Puget Sound. There are few other locally accessible opportunities to catch large and very strong fish on a fly rod. In addition, a number of easily accessible Puget Sound estuary locations have been discovered and subsequently popularized.

While chum salmon have been caught by fly anglers in open water, by and large this is uncommon. Chum salmon are most accessible in estuaries or at the mouths of creeks or rivers. While Chum runs occur from September to November, in the Hood

Chico Creek estuary is a good example of a healthy semi-urban estuary. Parts of its watershed have been rehabilitated to enhance salmon access and spawning areas. Chico Creek harbors a substantial Chum run, as well as growing Coho and native sea-run cutthroat trout populations.

Canal and a number of other locations there are summer-run Chum that start to show as early as July. Summer-run Chum tend to be more slender than fall-run Chum and hold their silver color longer. When hooked they also jump more than hard-charging fall Chum. Hood Canal Quilcene River estuary summer Chum are coincident with a voluminous hatchery Coho salmon run. These occur late July to early August. Because of seriously declining numbers, Hood Canal summer Chum were listed under the Endangered Species Act. They were subsequently closed to angling to assist in their recovery.

Chum salmon are most often reticent to take a quickly stripped fly. Place your cast far enough ahead of schools of fish so that the sinking fly will be just above or at eye level when intercepted by the school.

The simple techniques effective in catching Chum have not changed much over the years. A floating line, long leader and a fluorescent chartreuse fly is most popular. Wakes of moving schools of fish are often visible. A fly fished dead slow in front of a moving school is all it takes to have a chance to hook one of these leviathans. In deeper estuary waters, sink-tips or intermediate sinking lines may be useful.

Pink Salmon

Beaches, Estuaries, Bays, and Terminal Inlets

When the Pink salmon are running, my fly-fishing cohorts and I hit the beaches for a most exciting inshore fly-fishery. Large Pink runs occur every other year, the odd year in Puget Sound. Pinks tend to run in schools along shorelines when they get close to their spawning streams. Likewise, I have seen very large schools of surfacing Pinks in island inlets near the northeastern side of Vancouver Island. But it is their beach-running behaviors that make them a more ideally accessible game fish to the wading fly angler.

Some thirty-five years ago I was living in Port Alice on the north end of Vancouver Island. Friend, neighbor and fishing partner Martin Tolley of British Columbia steelhead fame discovered a most productive local beach to take Pinks on a fly. The beach was a spit at the mouth of the Cluxewe River. Cluxewe Pink runs are strongest on even numbered years. The Cluxewe River is still famous for several species of salmon as is the nearby Keogh River.

Aaron O'Brien with a beautiful Pink salmon caught off a Puget Sound beach.

Point no Point in northern Puget Sound also provides an excellent odd-year Pink fishery. Alaskan favorites of mine are beaches on the Kodiak road system adjacent to river estuaries including Salt Creek, Russian River, American River and Olds River. These estuaries are easily accessible by paved road from the town of Kodiak.

Pinks are vulnerable to small patterns like Wheenies dressed with UV Krystal Flash. Also effective are small and very sparsely dressed reflective baitfish patterns like the Pink Fly. Some fly anglers have enticed Pinks to take a small float-ing fly like the Mini Gurgler or a small Miyawaki Popper. Pink salmon are adapted to see UV colors better than most other species of salmon, possibly with the exception of Sockeye. This may be because UV colors are often pre-dominant in the ocean zooplankton that they feed on much of their lives. It is useful to include a small amount of blue or purple winging material and/or UV Krystal Flash in Pink fly dressings.

Because of their smaller size, three to six pounds, Pink salmon are fun on a six-weight fly rod. A floating line is most often adequate but sink-tip lines also work well when fishing wet flies. However, where Pink runs coincide with Coho runs it may not be a bad idea to upsize to a seven-weight or eight-weight rod.

Sockeye Salmon

Estuaries, Bays, and Terminal Inlets

Sockeye salmon have to be one of the best-fighting salmon, bar none. Their runs and aerial gyrations can be nothing less than spectacular. A favorite Sockeye destination of mine is Saltery River estuary. This estuary is acces-sible by float plane, one of several local fishing lodges or via very rough and sometimes dangerous 18-mile ATV trail to the back side of Kodiak Island. Individual fish in this particular run range from six to nine pounds. They readily take a green or fluorescent chartreuse fly. A particularly effective fly is simply a small piece of green yarn tied to a size-4 Gamakatsu Octopus hook. Alternatively, small Chartreuse or green Clousers can be very effec-tive, especially if UV materials are incorporated.

It is best to target schools as they run into the mouth of the river on the incoming tidal saltwater wedge. Once they get into a river Sockeye can become frustratingly closed mouthed. Drop a fly in front of a moving school and the second or third fish in the school most often takes, rarely the lead fish.

> Sockeye salmon are most vulnerable when they are running into the mouth of a river. They most often run with the salt wedge on an incoming tide. While the lead fish in the school will rarely take a fly, the second or third fish often will.

Intercepting Sockeye in outer estuaries or bays is uncommon. But there are exceptions. I fished the back side of Kagalaska Island, an island located next to Adak Island far down in the Aleutian chain several seasons running. There was a small un-named estuary on the Pacific Ocean side of the island. The estuary was accessible by boat in fair weather from the Adak Island Navy base which is now closed. The seas can be very rough in this area. It was necessary to run through a three-mile passage between Adak Island and Kagalaska Islands, from Bearing Sea to the Pacific Ocean. The sockeye would come in by the thousands. They staged in front of a very small creek that led out of a lake several hundred yards upstream. Kagalaska sockeye readily took a Fluorescent Green Wheenie fished dead slow on a floating line.

Ted Teather

A beautiful Kodiak Island salmon resting on a bed of seaweed.

Mark Salo with a Saltery Sockeye.

I am also aware that a few Vancouver Island fly anglers effectively target these fish from boats in Alberni Inlet, British Columbia. In any case, Sockeye feed primarily on large zooplankton. Most imitations should reflect this. Like Pinks, Sockeye are adapted to seeing UV colors well. Therefore, it is useful to include green to violet and UV colors in fly patterns.

A fly-angler wading the shallows in search of Sockeye off the mouth of the Saltery River, Kodiak Island, Alaska.

4

Putting It All Together: Designing Effective Salmon Flies

"The sound of masses of baitfish becoming airborne attempting to escape marauding salmon is unforgettable. It is a distinctive rushing sound, like soft but heavy rain. 'Shooooosh....' Thousands of baitfish jumping out of the water is what makes the sound. The phenomenon reminds me of waves of people raising and lowering their hands during a baseball game. Once you have heard the sound of panicked baitfish fleeing from salmon feeding along shorelines, you will never forget it. It's like wind or the rustling of leaves, as thousands of individuals exit the water in a constant volley. It is the sound of flight from certain death."

—Stoll, 2004

In saltwater fly fishing "matching the hatch" is not always a simple matter of copying form and color of the prey. Effective flies most often imitate significant prey characteristics that incite fish to react. These characteristics imitate the disturbance a fly makes in the water, how materials act in the water, and colors within the limited visual color perception of salmon. Fishing methods and fly designs are most often inseparable. Ideally they should be uniquely adapted to each other.

Salmon prey may also include, depending on life stage, invertebrates such as euphausids and other members of the decapod family, various flat and round worms, and free-swimming larval stages of crabs and other crustaceans. Salmon appear to key in on either body movement, how the prey moves through the water, fluorescence, blue to ultraviolet colors, or some combination of these factors. Attention to these types of details is important in the construction of effective flies.

For those flies that incorporate fluorescent materials an adequate level of ambient light is important to allow these materials to fluoresce. Best are fluorescent materials within the limited colors that salmon see best. Fluorescent chartreuse falls into this category. Fluorescent chartreuse emits the most light of any of the fluorescent colors and at greater depths. From personal experience there is little doubt that under the right conditions, light-emitting materials can greatly enhance the effectiveness of a fly.

A word of caution: some fly-tying materials marked as fluorescent are either not fluorescent or are only marginally fluorescent. This can be easily tested in the dark under inexpensive blue or black light bulbs that are available in most hardware stores. A fluorescent bulb appears to work better than an incandescent bulb. This is important because some fly designs are only effective because they are fluorescent. For example, the Fluorescent Chartreuse Clouser described in this section is effective because of its fluorescence. Salmon have a very low visual sensitivity to non-fluorescent chartreuse but a very high visual sensitivity to fluorescent chartreuse.

Factors in Fly Design

Use the Right Fly for the Situation

An astute fisherman once told me that he could tell a good fly angler by the number of flies in his or her fly box. If the fly box is stuffed with a myriad of types and sizes of flies it is likely is that the angler simply does not know what to use. When targeting resident Coho, appropriate flies should be of a relatively small size and fished near or on the surface. Likewise, on sunny days one should have a few flies that sink a little deeper. There are other important considerations.

Five Basic Principles of Fly Design

Fly designs should consider any or all of the following factors:

1. Color: The actual color as the fish sees it
2. Vibration: The waves a fly makes either under or on top of the water
3. Reflection: How they reflect light in the water
4. Silhouette: how visible the fly is against a background
5. Footprint: The impression the fly makes under the water or on the water surface

Color Is Not Always A Dominating Factor

Stick with colors that salmon can see best unless colorful flies tickle your fly fishing fancy. Bright colors, including pink, yellow and orange, may be only visible to salmon in clear shallow waters; sometimes effectively, especially for Pinks. Fly color is of little consequence when the fly is silhouetted against the sky. Fluorescent colors are much more visible to salmon deeper in the water column. Blues and greens are visible to salmon at all fly-angling depths so long as there is adequate light. Likewise, ultraviolet materials are more visible to salmon. However, red often provides a strong silhouette against the blues and greens of the underwater seascape even though the color red is often not visible to salmon.

Water Disturbances Emulating Swimming Baitfish Should Be A Consideration

Salmon appear to respond to baitfish movement through sensing movement through the lateral line. Fly designs including variations of the Coho Special and the Miyawaki Popper capitalize on water disturbances that emulate baitfish. This attribute, combined with materials that are mobile in the water, can be very effective in eliciting a response from salmon.

Flash Can Often Be the Key

Anglers have long known that flashy materials attract salmon. The silver sides of baitfish fleeing from predators create a lot of flash. This excites a salmon's feeding response. Likewise, as salmon twist and turn in pursuit of baitfish their own silver sides flash. This feeding flash likely draws other salmon. Terminal-tackle anglers who troll large flashers in front of baits will attest to increased hooking success. There are situations where too much flash can be a deterrent. There have been situations where I have found that removing some of the flashy material from a fly has increased its effectiveness.

Salmon May Also Target Eyes

The incorporation of eyes into baitfish patterns may at times increase their effectiveness. Throughout nature there are numerous examples where eyes are important in prey and predator interactions. Most tropical saltwater sport fish appear to key in on baitfish eyes. This also may be the case for salmon, but to some lesser degree. Even though salmon have relatively poor visual acuity it seems logical to include disproportionately large eyes on some baitfish imitations.

Salmon Feed Most Actively During Low-Light Conditions

While salmon appear to feed during peak periods in any 24-hour day, mornings and evenings are the optimal times for fly anglers. Most salmon species tend to move deeper into the water column during intense sunlight hours.

Many baitfish and invertebrate prey species move deeper in the water column in bright light. Mornings and evenings are closer to the lower light conditions that both salmon and their prey often prefer. These are also the times when salmon are no longer able to detect colors very well. During low-light conditions dark flies often cast the most highly visible silhouette.

Fly Patterns that Catch Salmon

The limited numbers of fly patterns contained herein have been proven to be effective for Pacific salmon. Each takes some of the above factors and salmon behavioral observations discussed in this book into consideration.

Coho Special

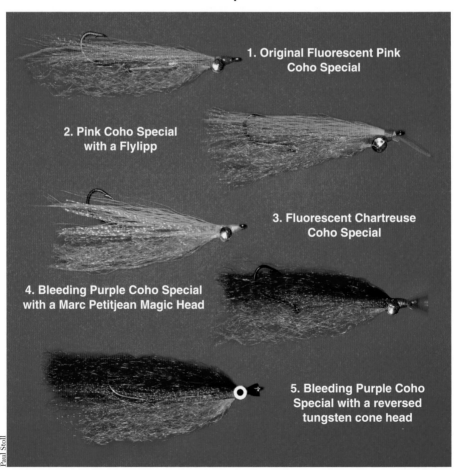

1. Original Fluorescent Pink Coho Special

2. Pink Coho Special with a Flylipp

3. Fluorescent Chartreuse Coho Special

4. Bleeding Purple Coho Special with a Marc Petitjean Magic Head

5. Bleeding Purple Coho Special with a reversed tungsten cone head

Paul Stoll

The Coho Special and its variations were created to take advantage of as many significant characteristics as possible. Colors are those that salmon see well. These include blues, purples, ultraviolet tones and fluorescent chartreuse and pink. Wing materials have a live action in the water. The fly is weighted with barbell eyes or a tungsten cone head. This original pink version takes advantage of both fluorescence and UV materials. These enhance its visibility to salmon. The Coho Special incorporates a barbless trailing hook which increases hooking ability, easy release, and prevents the materials from getting tangled in the bend of the hook when casting.

Originator: Richard Stoll
Tier: Richard Stoll

Hook &Body: Mustad 34007 or equivalent, sizes 2-4 (cut off above bend on completion of the fly).

Thread: Danville 210 denier Flat Waxed Nylon, color to match.

Stinger: Red Gamakatsu Octopus, size 4, snelled or looped with Hi-Vis Red Amnesia monofilament. The stinger is fastened to the body hook so in the completed fly it will be a fraction shorter than the length of the wing (Figure 4-1). This helps prevent wing materials from wrapping around the stinger hook while casting.

Wing & Belly: UV light purple or UV white Deadly Dazzle.

Lateral Line: UV pink Krystal Flash.

Overwing: Fluorescent pink bucktail.

Coho Special Variations

The following variations of the Coho Special take advantage of as many significant characteristics as possible. Colors are those that salmon see well. These include blues, purples, ultraviolet tones and fluorescent chartreuse. Wing materials have a live action in the water. Three of the listed variations use a reversed tungsten cone head open side forward, a Marc Petitjean Magic Cone Head, or a Flylipps scoop. These create water disturbances intended to emulate those of swimming baitfish. Flylipps can be turned up or down relative to the barbell eyes. This will cause the fly to either ascend or dive when stripped.

Pink Coho Special with a Flylipps

Head: A Flylipps is tied before the barbell eyes. Flylipps have a grooved extension designed to fit hook shanks (www.flylipps.com).

Fluorescent Chartreuse Coho Special

Wing &Belly: UV light purple or UV white Deadly Dazzle.

Lateral Line: Fluorescent chartreuse Krystal Flash.

Overwing: Fluorescent chartreuse bucktail.

Bleeding Purple Coho Special with a Marc Petitjean Magic Head

Head: A Petitjean Magic Head is slipped over the hook before the barbell eyes are tied on (www.petitjean.com).

Wing & Belly: UV light purple or UV white Deadly Dazzle.

Lateral Line: Fluorescent purple Krystal Flash.

Overwing: Farrar's Bleeding Purple Flash Blend or equivalent.

Bleeding Purple Coho Special With A Reversed Tungsten Cone Head

Head: A tungsten cone is slipped over the hook and position with a knot of tying thread in front so that it is positioned just behind the eye of the hook.

Wing & Belly: UV light purple or UV white Deadly Dazzle.

Lateral line: fluorescent blue or purple Krystal Flash.

Overwing: Farrar's Bleeding Purple Flash Blend or equivalent.

Wheenies

This fly was designed for terminal Coho salmon incorporating ideas my former fly-fishing shop partner, Bob Searle, was experimenting with during the early 1990's. Significant characteristics are the fluorescent chartreuse body in the form of Dungeness crab megalops larvae. However, this fly imitates the general characteristics of many types of larger plankton species. Wheenies can be extremely effective for terminal Coho off the feed. Smaller-sized, six and eight, Wheenies often illicit a response when terminal salmon are reticent to pick up larger versions. I have taken several bright Coho salmon of approximately eighteen pounds on a size-eight Fluorescent Green Wheenie.

Fluorescent Green Wheenie

Bill Thompson

The fly should be fished with the "amphipod hop" described in *Fly Fishing for Pacific Salmon II* (Johnson, et. al., 2008). This is several short quick strips followed by a pause to let the fly fall. This fly is also very effective for Pink and Chum salmon.

Originator: Richard Stoll
Tier: Richard Stoll

Hook: Gamakatsu SC-15, size 4-8, or equivalent or a red octopus hook, size 4-6.

Feelers: Fluorescent chartreuse or UV purple Krystal Flash contiguous with shellback and beard. Attach as a bunch in front of the eyes before making the body. After the fly is tied clip out all but two two-inch feelers, the remaining clipped Krystal Flash extending one quarter inch beyond the bend of the hook. Save the clipped bunch for the next fly.

Body: Black mono eyes are tied in first. Tie in the silver Mylar tinsel for the under-body. Fluorescent chartreuse V-rib is wrapped over the tinsel to the eye of the hook. Immediately in front of the eyes the Krystal Flash butts from the feelers are brought forward for a shellback and tied in at the eye of the hook.

Beard: Krystal Flash, continuous with the feelers and shellback tied forward under the fly.

Alternative: For the UV Pink Wheenie, substitute UV pink Ice dub for the body and UV Pink Krystal Flash for the feelers, shellback and beard.

UV Pink Wheenie

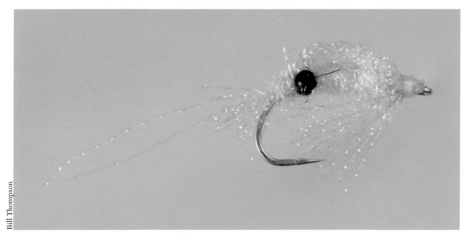

Bill Thompson

Mylar Baitfish

Bill Thompson

The original version of this fly was tied by Bob Searle in 1993. I made relatively minor modifications. Significant characteristics are the eyes, flash from the Mylar tubing, shape, and a hint of fluorescent red in the body created by a fluorescent Amnesia stiffener inside the Mylar tube body. This is an impressionistic fly. It is meant to imitate a generic baitfish that has been injured.

This fly is not designed to be quickly stripped like feather- or hair-dressed streamers. It should be fished on a floating or sink-tip line. Allow the fly to fall and drift in the current or in and around schools of candle-fish, herring, or smelt. If action is needed to illicit a strike, make a few short strips, letting the fly fall between strips. This fly will most often be picked up between strips.

Originator: Bob Searle
Tier: Richard Stoll

Hook: Daiichi 2546 stainless, sizes 1-6, or equivalent, de-barbed. I sometimes use a red Gamakatsu octopus hook.

Tail/Body: 5/32" Pearl Mylar tubing. Remove the string from the tubing and flatten with an iron just warm enough so as not to fuse the Mylar. A hen or similar hackle section is super-glued inside the tube as a tail-fin.Use Zip-Kicker to instantly set the super glue. A de-barbed hook is threaded through the tubing. A piece of 25-pound fluorescent red Amnesia is threaded down the center of the Mylar tubing and tied in along with the tubing at the head.

Wing: Blue and green bucktail mixed in equal parts or another suitable alternative, sparse, two-thirds the length of the Mylar tubing.

Eyes: Wapsi doll eyes or 5/32" pearl stick-on dome eyes. Fill around the eyes with super glue and set with Zip-Kicker.

Angel Hair Candlefish

Bill Thompson

One of the original versions of this fly was tied in 1996 by Glenn Starr, a commercial fly tier in Poulsbo, WA. Significant characteristics are the shape, eyes, and a very mobile Angel Hair body. The use of purple and/or ultraviolet materials in the fly significantly enhances its effectiveness. This is an impressionistic fly meant to closely imitate a baitfish.

This fly can be quickly stripped like a feather-dressed streamer or slowly stripped like the Mylar Candlefish. It can be fished on a floating line, intermediate line, or a sink-tip. Often effective is allowing the fly to fall and drift in the current in and around schools of candlefish. If action is needed to illicit a strike, then try a few quick short strips then allowing the fly to fall.

Originator: Glenn Starr
Tier: Richard Stoll

Hook: Daiichi 2546 stainless, sizes 2 to 8, or equivalent.

Wing: Overwing: Peacock or brown green or violet Angel Hair. Underwing: A few strands of ultraviolet Krystal Flash and white or pearl Angel Hair. The wing is tied in at the head and extended well past the bend of the hook.

Head: Small braided pearl Mylar tubing slipped on over the Angel Hair and tied off at the head with white thread. Color the top of the Mylar tubing with an olive green or brown Prismcolor pen. Add small stick-on flat eyes and coat the entire head with 5-minute epoxy. The fly should be turned until the epoxy is set.

Miyawaki Popper

Bill Thompson

The Miyawaki Popper was created by Leland Miyawaki, angler extraordinaire and a manager in the Orvis fly fishing shop in Bellevue, Washington. This fly is designed to create a wake in the surface reminiscent of an injured or fleeing baitfish. The reversed foam popper head creates wakes that radiate out over the water surface. The Icelandic sheep hair that makes up the bulk of the wing is very "live" in the water. Color is not particularly important as is the case with most floating flies and poppers that are viewed from below.

The Miyawaki Popper has a proven record as a top producer for feeding Coho salmon but also Pink salmon. Coho salmon will surface behind the fly and follow it, dorsal fin out of the water. Miyawaki gives an excellent description on how to fish this fly in *Northwest Fly Fishing* (Miyawaki, 2006). The Miyawaki Popper is a most exciting fly to fish.

> **Originator**: Leland Miyawaki
> **Tier**: Leland Miyawaki
>
> **Hook**: Mustad 3407, size 6 for the body, cut off at the bend after completion of the fly. The stinger is a Gamakatsu Octopus, size 4.
>
> **Head**: Rainey's Pee-Wee pop or Mini-Me pop reversed with the cupped side facing back.
>
> **Tail**: Silver holographic Flashabou, mixed-color Krystal Flash, Icelandic sheep, (white and olive), peacock hurl.
>
> **Hackle**: Grizzly or pink, one feather on each side.

Pete's Popper

Bill Thompson

This fly was first tied by Peter Penardi in 1984 while working in my former Poulsbo, Washington fly fishing shop. It was designed for fishing smaller resident Coho salmon. This fly is highly effective because of the small size and because it creates a wake on the surface reminiscent of a fleeing baitfish.

Originator: Peter Penardi
Tier: Richard Stoll

Hook: Gamakatsu SS-15 or equivalent, size 6 or 8.

Tail: Pearl deadly dazzle with a few strands of pearl Krystal Flash.

Head: Spun white deer body hair cut to shape.

Mini Gurgler

Bill Thompson

The Mini Gurgler was one of a series of flies originated by the late Jack Gartside. Like Pete's Popper, the Mini Gurgler is designed to fish on the surface for resident Coho salmon. It is effective because of the small size and the wake it creates on the water surface.

Originator: Jack Gartside
Tier: Richard Stoll

Hook: Gamakatsu SS-15 or equivalent, size 6 or 8.

Tail: Few strands of pearl Krystal Flash.

Body: Pearl Krystal Chenille.

Shell: White foam sheeting cut to shape, tied in at the tail, and brought forward to the head after the body is tied in.

Hackle: Small mallard breast feather.

Fluorescent Chartreuse Mirage Clouser

Bill Thompson

This fly form was originated by well-known angler and fly designer Bob Clouser and is described in his excellent book, *Clouser's Flies: Tying And Fishing the Fly Patterns of Bob Clouser* (Clouser, 2006). In its many modifications, sizes, and colors it has been one of the best fish-producers ever designed. In my opinion, the single characteristic that makes this fly so unique are the barbell eyes tied on top of the hook. This causes the hook to ride upside down. This can help prevent snagging on the bottom in shallower waters. Its effectiveness is also because the fly sinks very quickly thereby covering more of the water column.

Significant characteristics of the Chartreuse Mirage version are fluorescence and flash. Flashabou Mirage tinsel is one of the most light-reflective of fly-tying materials. The addition of ultraviolet Krystal Flash as an overwing can also be effective. To give this fly more action, one can add a Flylipp tied either in the up or down position.

Originator: Bob Clouser
Tier: Richard Stoll

Hook: Daiichi 2546 stainless, sizes 1/0-6, or equivalent.

Eyes: Barbell metal tied on top about 1/8 to 1/4 inches behind the eye of the hook.

Underwing: Fluorescent chartreuse bucktail with a chartreuse mirage topping both tied in front and in back of the barbell eyes. A few strands of UV Krystal Flash may be added.

Overwing: While bucktail the same length as the overwing, tied in at the underside of head.

For shallow water and/or dry-line fishing shallow water, tie the same fly substituting fluorescent pink bucktail for the chartreuse bucktail and add some UV pink Krystal Flash as a center line. This fluorescent pink version can be extremely effective for both juvenile and in-migrating adults running close to beaches.

A nice Coho taken on a Chartreuse Clouser Minnow.

Chum Candy

There are many local variations of Chum Candy. In my opinion, this is one of the more effective variations. This version incorporates purple hackle and strands of UV Krystal Flash in the tail. This fly is effective because it incorporates materials which are highly visible to Chum salmon. Chum flies should be fished very slowly on a floating or slow-sinking line. If the fly is picked by a fish it will likely be the second or third fish in the school, rarely the lead fish.

Bill Thompson

Originator: Unknown
Tier: Richard Stoll

Hook: Size 1/0 to 4 stainless.

Tail: Fluorescent chartreuse marabou, tied heavy, the length of the hook shank. A few strands of UV Krystal Flash.

Body: Fluorescent chartreuse chenille.

Hackle: Purple schlappen.

Alien

This fly is an adaptation by Ted Teather, a fly-fishing instructor at Peninsula Outfitters in Poulsbo, Washington. The significant characteristics of this fly are the heavy barbell eyes which enable it to sink quickly, dark colors that Chinook seem to prefer, and a long mobile tail. This fly was designed specifically for Chinook salmon staging in relatively shallow water before running into Miller Bay, a central Puget Sound inlet but is generally effective in a variety of situations where a fast-sinking dark fly is needed.

Originator: Ted Teather
Tier: Richard Stoll

Hook: 2/0 to 2 stainless.

Tail: Black or purple bunny strips overlaid with a few strands of UV Krystal Flash.

Bill Thompson

Body: Black or purple chenille with a palmered black or purple schlappen hackle.

Head: Large lead barbell eyes wrapped over with fluorescent chartreuse chenille.

The author in the Olds River estuary with a bright Coho salmon of approximately 18 pounds, Kodiak Island, Alaska.

Lloyd Powell

Pink Fly

This fly was designed for pink salmon. Pink salmon prefer small flashy flies reminiscent of baitfish. This fly incorporates blue, green, and UV colors that Pinks are best adapted to see.

Bill Thompson

Originator: Richard Stoll
Tier: Richard Stoll

Hook: 2-6 stainless 4XL.

Body: White wool overlaid by gold Mylar tinsel with an oval silver rib.

Wing: Blue and green bucktail mixed, sparse, overlaid with UV pink Krystal Flash.

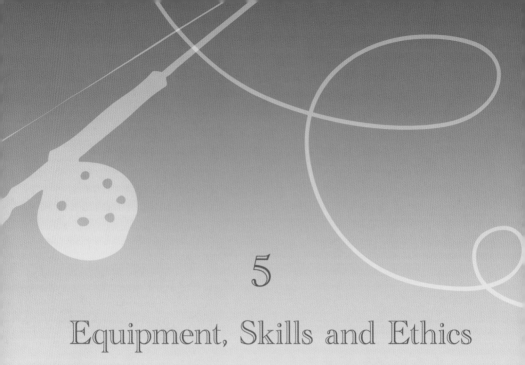

5

Equipment, Skills and Ethics

"Along the shores of Puget Sound, preparation for the emergence of spring is as old as human habitation. This preparation starts with the onset of winter and fills cool months with activity. Amongst anglers of both ancient and present generations, this has come in the form of building and mending equipment in anticipation of a new angling year."

—Stoll, 2002

Equipment and Skills

Fly-fishing shops and sporting goods stores are replete with rods, reels, and lines. Getting the right equipment for the job can be particularly confusing to even moderately experienced anglers. As important as having the right equipment is one's ability to skillfully use that equipment. Skills and equipment go hand in hand. The most inexperienced of fly-anglers will not be able to efficiently cast the best designed and balanced fly rod. Likewise, an experienced angler will not be able to efficiently cast a poorly designed fly rod or with the wrong-weight fly line. Balance in this case means having the right-weight fly line on a well-designed rod.

This section is not meant to be definitive. Rather it is to lay out some general guidelines for the selection of equipment suitable for fly fishing for salmon in inshore salt waters. If you are not sure about what to purchase, consult an expert. It is best to go to fly-fishing specialty shops for advice. While well meaning, many sporting goods store clerks are not expert in fly fishing methods or equipment.

Rods

A high-quality fly rod balanced to the right fly line is the single-most important fly-angling tool. High quality does not necessarily mean the most expensive rod. There are many well designed but relatively inexpensive rods that function very well for both novice and expert alike.

Many modern fly anglers like to use the lightest rod possible. They imagine that this is a more challenging way to catch fish. But this can lead to far more challenging casting issues. Light-weight rods require light-weight fly lines to cast efficiently. Light-weight fly lines will not efficiently carry larger and heavier flies no matter how good a caster one may be. If the fly is not weightless as compared to weight of the line, casting becomes exceeding difficult regardless of the quality of the rod. This can be very frustrating indeed, especially for those with modest casting abilities.

A seven-to nine-weight rod is ideal for most salmon fishing conditions with the exception of smaller resident salmon. Rods that are approximately nine feet in length create the leverage needed for easier long casts. Some saltwater salmon fly anglers have started using 10 1/2- to twelve-foot switch rods. These rod lengths were traditionally built from heavy materials and used for two-handed overhead or Spey casts. However, many modern light-weight switch rods can be cast single-handed like a shorter rod.

Paul Stoll

Excellent saltwater rods come in a number of makes and models and in a wide range of prices. The above are three examples. Left to right (2010 prices): 9' 8wt Sage XI3 ($700.00); 9'6" 7wt Redington CPX ($329.95); 9' 8wt TFO Professional ($149.95).

A high-quality switch rod in the hands of a reasonable fly-caster enables more distance with fewer false casts.

Fly Lines

High-quality fly lines are important for most saltwater salmon fly fishing situations. I prefer to use weight-forward floating lines whenever I can. Where depth does not allow a floating line, sink-tip or full-sinking lines are useful. When fishing cold waters it is expedient to use a line designed for cold water. Warm-water lines and many inexpensive lines will hold a set in cold waters. Coils will get hung up in the guides during casting. No matter what make or model of line, most important is that it balances the rod. Otherwise, casting will become most difficult. If one is unsure about fly lines, a fly fishing professional should be consulted.

Reels

Salmon reels should be saltwater resistant. Most good-quality reels are made of anodized aluminum or carbon fiber. Moving parts are made of metals that do not corrode or react with the aluminum body of the reel when exposed to salt water. If they are not, saltwater-facilitated galvanic reaction will result in the finish flaking off and the surface of the aluminum turning to powder. Years ago this happened to my older-model Hardy reels. They were fine reels but they were painted or powder-coated aluminum.

A smooth drag is important. A smooth drag lightly set should not allow the reel to overrun when the line is sharply pulled. The drag should have a nearly imperceptible point of inertia. The point of inertia is the point of drag engagement when line is pulled off the reel. Most modern mid-range priced fly reels have relatively well-designed drags.

Good reels should stand up in salt water indefinitely given a little care.
The Charleton Signature Series above has given me flawless service
during many hundreds of hours of fishing over the past 15 years.

Above are some of the many excellent reels available in fly fishing shops. Top:
Left to right (2010 prices): Lamson Konic 3.5 ($139.00), Ross CLA 4 ($230.00);
Bottom: Sage 3880 CF ($280.00, Galvin T-8 $400.00), Tibor Everglades (640.00).

Regardless of quality, after use in salt water all reels should be thoroughly rinsed with fresh water. If not, even in the best of reels, salt crystals can form in tight joints and between running surfaces. A good practice is to strip the fly line off while in the shower after a fishing trip. Thoroughly rinse the reel before winding the fly line back on.

Casting

Casting in salt waters can be very challenging at times. This is particularly true during the prevalent windy conditions along saltwater beaches on the Straights of San Juan de Fuca, Salish Sea, inner Puget Sound, as well as many other salmon-bearing coastal waters.

Casting directly into the wind can be made easier by lowering your casting stroke close to the water. This is sometimes difficult when there are banks, rip rap, or vegetation behind. In these cases a good command of the double-haul will add a great deal of speed and momentum to the fly line. This increases your ability to penetrate onshore winds with shorter and higher back casts.

When a cross wind is blowing toward the casting hand the fly line will often blow into the angler. This creates the danger of hooking one's self. Try turning around and casting backwards. There is very little difference between forward and back casts. With a little practice casting backward can be as easy as casting forward.

The author giving advanced fly-casting lessons and coaching at Trophy Lakes Golf and Casting Club in Port Orchard, Washington. Even relatively proficient fly-casters can use a periodic tune-up.

While most salmon are taken relatively close to shore, long casts cover more water. Even if one is already a reasonable caster there is always a good case for obtaining coaching from an expert. Don't be shy to do so. Superstars like golfer Tiger Woods, as well as many champion fly-casters, employ coaches at times. Whenever possible get coaching from a Federation of Fly Fishers-certified casting instructor. These people are not only good casters but are expert in methods for coaching good casters and teaching novice casters.

The author executing a strong double-haul while fishing for salmon. The double-haul increases line speed which penetrates wind better and enables a much longer cast to cover more water.

Eight Simple Tips That Will Improve Your Fly-Casting

(1) Keep your elbow well below your chest. High-sticking your casts, as many fly-anglers tend to do, makes the angler wave the rod in an arc rather than propel the cast in a straight line. Further, holding the arm up high quickly causes arm fatigue. This leads to deteriorated casting.

(2) Minimize "breaking" your wrist during the casting stroke. The rod should be an extension of the lower arm. Casting from the hand and wrist causes the rod to wave in an arc and leads to inefficient casting. It also causes fatigue.

(3) Don't try to muscle the cast. Relax. More muscle does not make a cast go further. Trying harder does not make the cast better, but it does make tailing loops and wind knots. Fly-casting is an act of coordination and technique, not muscle.

(4) Let the line straighten out behind you. Starting the forward cast before the line straightens out has two effects. First, it snaps the line like a bull whip which can actually pop the fly off the leader. The snapping sound is the tip of the line exceeding the speed of sound. Second, your rod will not adequately load to produce an efficient cast. If necessary look over your shoulder to ensure the line straightens out before making your forward cast.

(5) Do not feed the line into the guides during the forward- or back-casting strokes. Many anglers do this without knowing it, even when they are holding the line tightly in the opposite hand. They allow the left hand to move forward during the forward-casting stroke. The rod will not load, and, therefore, not cast efficiently.

(6) Avoid the "anticipation" cast. The anticipation cast is when you decide to cast the line after often perfect false casts. Anglers tend to muscle the rod forward with great effort which often makes the cast fall apart. You should simply let the line release on one of those perfect false casts.

(7) Learn the double-haul. Even much abbreviated hauls can make short casts more efficient. But hauling can be hard to learn and takes some muscle memory. Have an expert show some exercises you can do while watching TV that will enable you to learn to double-haul very quickly.

⑧ Cast a fly line like you throw a football. Football players throw a football with a straight-arm trajectory over their shoulders, they release the ball at the end of the stroke. This makes the ball go in a straight line. The rod, the hand, the arm, and therefore the rod tip should also move in a substantially straight trajectory, not an arc, if the cast is to be efficient.

Wading

There seems to be a maxim among fly- and gear-anglers alike. "The fish are always located several feet further than the longest cast one can possibly make." One can observe this whenever amongst a diverse group of anglers. It seems that most will wade out to the top of their waders then make the longest cast possible. Truth be known, most fish are caught within 30 feet of the angler. I have often seen actively feeding Coho swim between me and the beach. Wade shallow, rarely more than knee deep. If tides are a factor in getting a fly where you want it, then fish lower tides.

A Modicum of Fishing Wisdom

There are two maxims that appear to govern the foundation of both still-water and stream fishing. These two maxims had eluded me until one fine angling morning on a local beach. A dozen or so anglers were braving the salt to the tops of their chest waders. Buzz-bomb throwers and fly-flingers alike were making Herculean casts that occasionally zinged past boats trolling some distance off shore.

A few dejected looking fly-anglers were nonchalantly loitering on the beach. The sullen looks on the faces indicated they were too embarrassed to fish among those with obviously greater physical ability and apparent long-standing angling expertise. How could they comfortably join the line-up with woefully inadequate casting abilities? Not a chance in a bait box did these pitiful individuals have amongst the far-flinging crowd of construction workers, weight-lifters, and marathon runners braving the depths in front of them.

Over the years I have observed these same phenomena on many other lakes, ponds, beaches and reservoirs. The first maxim popped into my head like an explosion:

"Fish always position themselves at least three feet further than the absolute longest cast by the very best caster."

Wind and waves often create challenging casting conditions.

In situations like that fateful morning on the beach any fish that is caught is purely incidental and, by the way, very dumb at that.

If this were true for beaches, then what about estuaries and sand spits? The answer was as obvious as the question. How many hundreds of times have I seen fly anglers also lining those shorelines, wading as deep as possible, then casting to the far side?

The issue is complicated when anglers are lined up along both sides of the body of water. Which side is the far side? This, of course, is simply a matter of perspective and depends on which side you are on. I remember once looking down the mouth of a river. Anglers lined both banks. Numerous lines were pulled taut across the river, many hooked together in the center by flies and lures. The second maxim popped into my head even faster than the first.

"Fish always position themselves along the far bank of any spit, bay, estuary, river, stream, or creek."

From the number of anglers I have seen behaving in this way, it is a wonder that I have not previously identified this most conventional of fishing wisdom.

Consider the thought:

"Having so little time, we think we must fish the best looking spots where everyone else fishes because they must be good or no one else would fish them. This is false reasoning because we are relying on precedents established by easy fishing and in most cases, by anglers who have followed the established rules rather than the dictates of their own minds."

—From Trout *by Ray Bergman.*

This brings me to sound advice for both angling and life in general.

"Wade a little shallower, cast a little shorter, and please do not step on the fish."

This last thought is a product of more than a half century of casting a fly.

On Ethics and Safety

The 15th century *A Treatyse on Fisshynge Wyth an Angle* by Dame Juliana Berners is the earliest known writing on the subject of fly-fishing (Berners, 1496). Dame Juliana was a prioress of Sopwell, they say a Nun, noblewoman, and sportswoman. Her treatise was published in *The Boke* [book] *of St. Albans*, a reference guide for training young gentlemen in falconry, heraldry, and hunting. Dame Juliana's advice is most surprising in light of sports ethics and conservation issues we face today.

On ethics:
"I charge that you break no man's hedges in going about your sports, nor open any man's gates without shutting them again. Also you must not use this aforesaid artful sport for covetousness, merely for the increasing of saving your money, but mainly for enjoyment and to procure the health of your body, and more especially, your soul."

On Conservation:
"Also you must not be too greedy in catching your said game, as in taking too much at one time, a thing that can easily happen if you do not in every point as this present treatise shows you. That could easily be the occasion of destroying your own sport and other men's also. When you have a sufficient mess [food], you should covet no more at that time. Also you should busy yourself to nourish the game in everything that you can do, and to destroy all things that are devourers of it."

For we saltwater fly-anglers other simple rules should apply:
- Always look behind you before making a cast. There may be bushes or other fly-eating obstructions, or worse yet a person in the path of your back cast.
- Share the beach. When there are other anglers present it is courteous to move along the beach to make room for others.

Pinch your hook barbs flat. In Puget Sound, barbless hooks are required. In any case there is less damage when you release a fish or when you try to pull the hook out of another person after an errant back cast.

- When casting always wear glasses to protect your eyes. Polarized lenses are most useful.

- Watch where you step. Beaches, bays and estuaries are full of living things.
- Respect private property rights. It is unfortunate that most beaches in Puget Sound, and many elsewhere, are not public. These beaches are the landowners' backyards.

6
Where to Fish

"Many men go fishing all of their lives without knowing that it is not fish they are after."… "Time is but the stream I go a-fishing in."

—Henry David Thoreau

Inner Puget Sound Beaches

Most salmon species can be taken along Puget Sound and other beaches at various times of the year, but most often in the late summer and fall. Many West Coast beaches are privately owned. They can only be accessed with the owners' permission. However, there are also many accessible public areas, road ends, and state and federal lands.

With some exceptions most Puget Sound beaches fish best on either side of a slack low tide; that is just before the low or just after the low when tidal velocity and other conditions are ideal. Bottom structure that holds prey is more accessible at low tides. And at lower tides anglers are not pushed back up onto a beach where brush or banks make casting difficult.

The inner Puget Sound beach access map (page 92) shows 12 of the more accessible areas. The Washington State Department of Ecology has an interactive web site with close-up aerial photos of all of these beaches. http://apps.ecy.wa.gov/shorephotos/

The beach at Salisbury Point on the Hood Canal, Puget Sound is a good location when the silvers are in. The Hood Canal floating bridge and the Olympic Mountains are in the background.

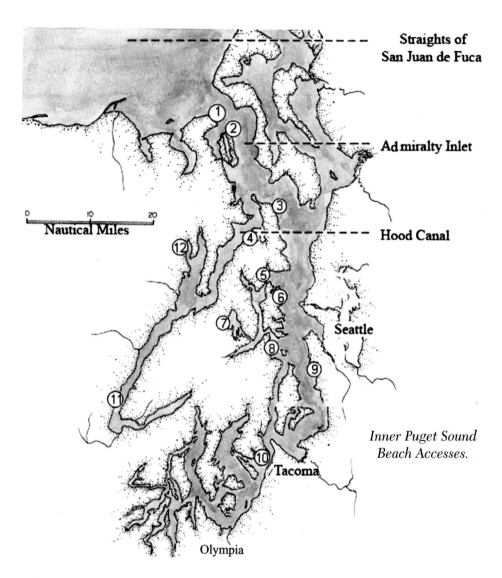

Inner Puget Sound Beach Accesses.

① **Location**: Point Wilson, Fort Worden State Park, Port Townsend.
   Species: Coho, incidental Chinook, odd-year Pinks.
   Timing: July to September.

② **Location**: Point Marrowstone, Fort Flagler State Park, Marrowstone Island.
   Species: Coho, incidental Chinook, odd-year Pinks.
   Timing: July to September.

③ *Location*: Point no Point County Park, Hansville.
Species: Coho, incidental Chinook, odd-year Pink
Timing: July to October.

④ *Location*: Salisbury Point County Park next to the
Hood Canal Floating Bridge.
Species: Coho.
Timing: July to September.

⑤ *Location*: Old Man Park, Suquamish.
Species: Coho.
Timing: September to October; juvenile Coho March through fall.

⑥ *Location*: Chico Creek Estuary, Dyes Inlet.
Species: Chum.
Timing: October to November.

⑦ *Location*: Fay Bainbridge State Park, Bainbridge Island.
Species: Coho, incidental Chinook.
Timing: August to November.

⑧ *Location*: Manchester State Park.
Species: Coho.
Timing: August to October; juvenile Coho, January through fall.

⑨ *Location*: Lincoln Park, Southwest Seattle.
Species: Coho.
Timing: August to October; juvenile Coho, January through fall.

⑩ *Location*: Tacoma Narrows Park, adjacent to the Tacoma
Narrows Bridge.
Species: Coho.
Timing: September to October; juvenile Coho December through summer.

⑪ *Location*: Finch Creek, Hoodsport, Hood Canal.
Species: Chum.
Timing: October to November.

⑫ *Location*: Quilcene Bay.
Species: Coho, Chum.
Timing: August to October.

Favorite Fishing Locations

Point no Point, Puget Sound

One of the most beautiful Kitsap County public beaches is the expanse of shimmering white sand that surrounds the Point no Point lighthouse. Point no Point, located at the northern point of Kitsap Peninsula in Washington State, also happens to be one of the few expanses of locally accessible beaches from which non-boat owners have a reasonable chance of catching mint-bright silver salmon.

Occasionally schools of silver salmon chase baitfish nearly up onto the beach. These fish are sometimes accessible even to the most inexperienced of anglers. At other times seals, many varieties of sea birds, and the occasional porpoise follow salmon and baitfish caught up in near-shore rip tides.

Until the last few years, Point no Point has been one the great-undiscovered beach-angling retreats in Puget Sound. But this year more anglers, picnickers, beach walkers, sightseers and wildlife aficionados than ever have been enjoying the amenities that the Point has to offer. The lighthouse and adjacent beaches are part of our public domain.

My family and I have enjoyed frequent fishing excursions to the Point. I have taken my share of salmon on a fly rod. I have watched others hook these silver treasures with all sorts of paraphernalia from flies to small buzz bombs to spoons. We all seem to share feelings of exclusivity for this beautiful location.

Not too long ago while fishing the early morning tide at Point no Point I heard something familiar. I instinctively turned toward the sound. Less than twenty feet from where I was standing a thousand baitfish were airborne i flight from predators. I had hit the beach at Point no Point in hopes that the resident Coho would be there as they normally are sometime after mid-May. Several small schools of fifteen- to eighteen-inch Coho were showing but not the schools of larger fish I was looking for.

Then, before my eyes, the ocean surface half a cast from where I was standing turned into a cauldron of frenetic activity. I could see the silver-blue flashes characteristic of blackmouth slashing through baitfish not more than twenty feet from where I was standing. Feeder Chinook, locally called blackmouth, often chase baitfish schools into water as shallow as four feet during low light early morning or late evening hours.

This particular early morning brought a blackmouth bonus, something that can happen in May and June. They were not showing in large numbers.

Blackmouth do not school like Coho. But small groups upwards of half a dozen fish were making forays onto a beach crowded with baitfish.

An even larger spring bonus can be the spring run of returning ocean Chinook, Springers, as they are called locally, can run in excess of twenty pounds. Hooking a salmon this large from a beach can be a real challenge. More than once in past springs I have been spooled by a Chinook I was not able to stop. No such luck that particular morning. But even more exciting, Point no Point can be prolific with resident Coho July through October. That is with a few resident blackmouth thrown in.

For both blackmouth and Coho ideal tidal velocities at the Point and elsewhere are between one and two knots. The incoming tide is best as it pushes baitfish and salmon up onto the beach. Tidal velocities should be checked before making the trip. Any location along the beach, from the parking lot to the Point can be good for Coho. Often rips will set up at or near the Point. Rip lines concentrate salmon prey. So fishing near, not in, a rip line can often be productive.

What: Coho, Pink Salmon
When: Mid-July to late October. Pink salmon in the odd years
Where: Point no Point beach, Hansville, Kitsap Peninsula, Washington State
Equipment: 7-8-wt. rod, floating or intermediate sink line, baitfish patterns

Chico Creek, Dyes Inlet, Puget Sound

"Many men fish to get away from women, but now they have to accept the galling reality that they can't escape." —*The New York Times*, Aug 8, 1994

Some call local chum fishing "picket fencing", others call it "combat fishing", but most call it fun fishing.

My wife, Ana, loves to fly-fish. She's not a Joan Wulff, the current Deaconess of the fly-casting world, but Ana can hold her own. Her graceful fifty-to sixty-foot casts put many macho slap-it-on-the-water male fly-anglers to shame. When salmon are on our beaches Ana is often more hot to trot than me. If she can convince me or a fly-fishing girlfriend she'll be off to locations like Point no Point in a flash.

"It's up to you if you want to come along," she'll inform me. "But I am not waiting. The tide is low and I have a good feeling."

One November Saturday afternoon not too long ago Ana was after me to go picket fencing for chum salmon at Chico Creek. Her justification was that the tides were right. Well, maybe she was not so much after me as after a

The Point no Point lighthouse is adjacent to one of the best white sand salmon angling beaches in the Puget Sound.

Paul Stoll

passel of new chum flies. She does not tie flies too often. I do. She was ready to go and I had better get hot at the fly-tying bench.

When we arrived things were "Chico Creek chum-run normal". There was hardly a place to park. Thirty-five or forty anglers were lined up knee-deep in the estuary like, you guessed it, a picket fence. They were all having a ball combat fishing.

This particular afternoon the line-up had formed a hundred-foot semi-circle around a pod of maybe 500 frightened chum salmon. Lures of every sort and kind were flying everywhere. Confused fish were rolling in futile attempts to miss the lure pandemonium. Three or four macho fly-anglers were among them. From the looks of things they had been taking fly-casting lessons from treble-hooked Buzz Bomb throwers.

A young lady of about 12 years of age squealed in delight as her rod doubled over from what looked like a dark purple-striped male hooked on some nether part of its anatomy. "Back up, back up!" her dad kept yelling. "That's a good smokin' fish. Don't you lose it!" The young lady squealed again then dutifully obeyed Dad's continuing spate of orders.

Ana looked at me and said, "Let's go down there, away from the crowd." She was pointing toward some shallows in the west end of the estuary where maybe twenty-five undisturbed fish were finning. Ana was off and fly-casting without even turning around to see if I had followed. I had not. I sometimes find it far more of a pleasure to watch her fish than to fish myself.

A couple of macho fly-anglers waded in near to where I was standing. One said, "Jeez! Look at that woman cast. Does she think she's trout fishing? I doubt if she will get anything on that wimpy outfit!" They had no idea she and I were soul mates.

The other macho fly-angler didn't respond. He looked at his partner with an expression that appeared halfway between agreement and mock disdain. He was obviously disgruntled at the thought of a graceful woman fly-angler going after Mac truck chum with what he obviously considered a "trout" rod. Just as he glanced back toward Ana she was fast into a substantial fish that she had legally hooked inside its mouth. She had a number more that afternoon, and more legally hooked fish than anyone else on the beach, including me.

In the car on our way back home Ana turned to me and asked, "Why didn't you fish very much? Then she followed her inquiry with, "Let's stop at the Silver City Brewery. Maybe you can tell me over a sandwich and a stout?"

I just smiled. It had been another wonderful angling afternoon.

I think it was in the early 1970's that I heard rumors of a few fly-anglers float tubing and catching gargantuan chum salmon at another location. This was off the mouth of the Finch Creek Hatchery in Hoodsport on the Hood Canal. The tip proved to be worthy indeed. One could get towed up and down beautiful Hood Canal October beaches by these fish. It took some years, but the sport caught on so well that it is still a planned annual migration for many anglers today.

In more recent years the chum salmon runs in Chico Creek estuary located on the southern shores of Dyes Inlet on the Kitsap Peninsula have recovered to the point where thousands of fall returning fish provide great sport for lots of anglers. This is where Ana and I most often go.

There is no trick to catching chum if one is a marginal fly-caster. Tie a fluorescent chartreuse Chum Candy onto the end of a 9-foot, 12-pound leader and a floating fly line. Cast the fly in front of a moving school of fish. Move the fly just enough to keep it off the bottom, no more. Wait for a bombshell.

What: Chum salmon
When: October to November
Where: Chico Creek estuary, Dyes Inlet, Bremerton, Washington State
Equipment: 8-wt. rod, floating line, fluorescent chartreuse flies

Puget Sound Resident Coho

It was nearly forty years ago that I first met Harry Lemire.

Without a doubt Harry was the most ardent and studied steelhead fly angler I ever had the privilege to associate with. There has hardly been a treatise on steelhead fly-angling that does not give him honorable mention, if not more. For this reason, twenty-some-odd years ago I was surprised when Harry told me he had temporarily abandoned winter steelhead fishing on the Green River. He was spending every spare moment fishing newly discovered resident Coho salmon in south Puget Sound.

As I remember, several years prior to Harry's disclosure, the Washington State Department of Fish and Wildlife discovered that many late-released hatchery Coho never left Puget Sound for their normal Pacific Ocean migrations. Department biologists decided to recreate a declining resident salmon sport fishery based on this fact.

The Department soon realized that 'time of release' was not the only factor that controlled salmon migration. Hence, the late-release strategy worked better in some years than others. Nevertheless, southern Puget Sound from Hartstein Island to Tacoma Narrows has become justifiably renowned for a December to April surface-water fishery for small Coho salmon.

A little-recognized phenomenon is that these salmon start moving north sometime in the early spring. Early to mid-April they show up in Sinclair Inlet and Bainbridge Island area from Washington Narrows to Lynwood Center, all central Puget Sound. In May they can usually be found between Point Monroe and Point no Point. June through November they scatter along beaches between Pilot Point and Port Ludlow, northern Puget Sound.

Resident Coho salmon grow considerably during this northward migration. In January, they weigh upwards of one pound. These same fish can attain four to six pounds by October. They reach sexual maturity in November. Many die without ever seeing a spawning stream.

Leland Miyawaki casting to Chums in Chico Creek Estuary. Chico Creek Estuary is highly productive for both Chum and Coho salmon.

Through late May resident salmon congregate in schools of 100 individuals or more to feed on plankton and small forage fish. Later in the season they abandon schooling behaviors and start feeding on candlefish and herring.

Schools of small Coho move quickly and often create surface commotion. To catch them it is necessary to position yourself within casting range of a school. The best way to do this is with a highly maneuverable small boat with a motor. Likewise, casting works better than trolling. If your fly-casting skills are up to speed, a fly-rod is ideal. A floating fly line will keep the fly up in the feeding zone. The trick is to cast to fish you can see breaking water.

I don't know if Harry still pursues resident Coho. He has returned to steelhead, other more exotic endeavors like pursuing tropical permit and bonefish and pursuing trout in New Zealand, but mostly tying presentation-class steelhead flies. As for me, I can't think of a better or more exciting Puget Sound fishery.

Photo courtesy of Ed Sozinho, Pro Image Photography, Inc.

What: Juvenile Coho salmon
Where: Puget Sound bays and beaches from Fox Island to Point no Point, Washington State
When: December to October following a northerly migration throughout these months
Equipment: 5-7-wt. rod, floating line, krill patterns and small poppers

Suquamish Beaches, Puget Sound

My fishing buddy and I descended down the steep path toward the cobble-stone beach below. We were about 200 feet above the water. From this vantage point we could see the full extent of the beach. Three salmon jumped along the stretch of beach immediately below us and another jumped a hundred yards to the south. "The fish are in!" I exclaimed.

We were at a beach under Agate Pass Bridge just south of Old Man Park in Suquamish. Suquamish is a quaint little town situated in the Port Madison Reservation about five miles east of Poulsbo, Washington. The waterfront affords beautiful views of the Seattle skyline. Every fall thousands of Coho salmon used to migrate south around Jefferson Head, past Indianola and head to Suquamish Tribe hatcheries and soon to newly reinstalled net pens.

My heart jumped again at what I saw on our final descent to the beach. My attention focused on a school of thirty or more salmon moving through water not more than six feet deep. The sight promised a spectacular afternoon, all the time I could afford in my busy work schedule. I had accepted an invitation from a friend, a local waterfront property owner, to park at his house. He asked that I stop for a cup of coffee and show him any salmon we caught on our return from the beach.

In a very short period of time, sometimes less than a month, returning Coho salmon such as these move from actively feeding on bait to not feeding at all. The same fish that we had first intercepted several weeks ago at Point no Point, then last week fished fornear Indianola dock on candlefish imitations, would not look at candlefish near Old Man Park in Suquamish. As salmon get close to their spawning destinations they simply stop feeding. Anglers must revert to attractor flies. The only thing that will consistently take these fish will be small fluorescent Chartreuse Green Wheenies fished very slowly.

It was an extraordinary afternoon. When we ascended the bank my friend was not home. He had left coffee on the front porch for us. In return I left a beautiful salmon I had meticulously cleaned with his kindness in mind.

What: Coho salmon
Where: Agate Pass both north and south of the bridge between
Bainbridge Island to Kitsap Peninsula
When: December to October following a northerly migration
throughout these months
Equipment: 5-7-wt. rod, floating line, krill patterns and small poppers

*The beach at Old Man House Park, Suquamish, Puget Sound. In
September and October salmon can be caught along this beach and
under the bridge in the background. The bridge leads to Bainbridge
Island on the left, location of the Sage Fly Rod factory.*

Neah Bay, Olympic Peninsula

It never ceases to amaze me how many fish can be found swimming beneath
the floating debris that accumulates along Puget Sound tide rips. My boat
was drifting along one of those rips, Coho salmon broke the surface both in
front of and behind us. Through my bronze-colored Polaroid glasses I saw
another fish flash beneath the surface.

We had motored out of Neah Bay earlier that August morning. Neah
Bay is on the Makah Indian Reservation hamlet at the northwestern tip of
Washington State. We were aware that schools of Coho salmon were provid-
ing some great fishing. We situated our boat several hundred yards east of

Duncan Rocks, small basalt protrusions in the mouth of the Straight of San Juan de Fuca.

An excited exclamation emanated from another boat 100 yards ahead of us. I looked up to see a double hook-up. Earlier I had noticed they were trolling very small blue-and-white Coho flies just under the surface. This is a very effective method for taking Coho under these conditions. Even though they had been fishing near us for nearly an hour, we had hooked three times the number of fish. This had not gone un-noticed. I could imagine their faith in what they were doing was dwindling.

Pete tied on another size-6 Mylar Baitfish. His had been shredded by three successive salmon and no longer tracked properly when he stripped it in. I was using one of my fluorescent shrimp imitations. Euphausids, the generic name of the crustacean my fly was imitating, are on the Coho salmon list of favorite foods. They had been taking it voraciously.

Pete's slow-sinking fly-line shot seventy feet from his fly-rod in a graceful loop. He was targeting a fish that had just broken the surface. Fly-casting to salmon in Puget Sound is very much like fly-casting to trout in a Montana river. All the same principles applied. Pete let his fly sink to about six feet below the surface. Pete stripped in the fly with short, quick pulls. The fish did not take. But the second cast was a charm. A beautiful mint-bright Coho of about eight pounds erupted from the water.

Ten minutes later I was leaning over the side of the boat to extract the barbless hook. Removing the fish from the water for even a short period of time might collapse the oxygen-absorbing structures in its gills, which often can be fatal. Neither Pete nor I had any intention of destroying this beautiful animal. I released the salmon without removing it from the water.

Later that evening at the boat ramp Pete and I reminisced over Thomas Kemper Root Beer and potato chips. How many thousands of people would have the opportunity to enjoy this wonderful resource if we would conserve it better? What a great economic and recreational benefit to the state if native Puget Sound Coho were managed primarily as a sport-fishing resource.

What: Coho salmon
Where: Neah Bay to Sekiu, northwest Olympic Peninsula Coast, Washington State
When: July to September
Equipment: 8-wt. rod, Intermediate or fast-sinking line, baitfish patterns

Quillayute, Olympic Peninsula

"Bob, get your fly in the water, there's a school coming your way," I shouted to my fishing partner standing thigh-deep in the river a hundred yards up stream. Polaroid glasses produced a crystal-clear shot of a thirty-plus school of Coho salmon. I looked downstream just in time to see a second school of approximately the same size charging up the tidewater into the river.

I had seen it like this before in the Quillayute. Starting about the first week of August Coho start to show in the lower Quillayute River where it meets the salt. Knowing this, we had come in anticipation of catching the first runs of the year. As it turned out we were right on.

My rod jerked as if someone had grabbed the line and yanked on it. I nearly lost my footing on the slick river bottom. I tightened my grip on the rod and spun around just in time to see an ocean-bright Coho break water, fluorescent orange-and-chartreuse fly tenuously perched in the edge of its white gum line. Then the tension on my rod relaxed as the fly dropped back to the river. I had been paying attention to Bob, not my fly rod. The fish was not well-hooked.

We were fishing the river from the Olympic National Park Mora campground, situated on tidal water. This is where the Quillayute River empties into the Pacific Ocean. During high tides the river adjacent to Mora campground essentially stops flowing. At low tide it becomes a river again. In-migrating fish enter the estuary on the high tide and quickly move up in the slack high-tide water to the Mora area. As the tide drops the fish are deposited in runs and riffles. Once this happens, they quickly charge upstream. Since they do not stick around, the idea is to catch them on the salt wedge within the first several hours after the tide starts to fall.

There is a great advantage to this strategy. Once Coho are in the river a day or two they become very reticent to take anything an angler presents. This often makes them very difficult to catch. But fresh out of the ocean they often take well.

Keys to successfully fishing Mora are to be there when the fish are there which, in part, means paying attention to the tides. If you have a Seattle-area tide log you must make the appropriate corrections for ocean tides. Then add an hour or two for upstream lag time. Most tide books have coastal-correction tables. The other trick is to be able to spot fish. This takes a good pair of Polaroid glasses. Had we not been spotting schools our chances of getting into these fast-moving fish would have been minimal.

Of course, fishing the tide is a crapshoot in any case. Fish migrate into the river when fish migrate into the river, which may not always be when one expects them to. All you can do is make accurate calculations. This makes a tide log a critical fishing tool.

What: Coho salmon
Where: Quillayute River adjacent to the Olympic National
Park Mora campground
When: August on a low to incoming tide
Equipment: 8-wt. rod, floating line, bright fly patterns

Afognak Island, Alaska

Mark and I waded knee-deep across a side channel carefully avoiding dozens of dead and dying Pink salmon. As we exited the water onto a large riverside meadow, the powerful stench of rotting fish and something else overwhelmed us.

The meadow was trashed. Waist-high Aleutian grasses had been trampled flat. Fly-infested fish carcasses were strewn everywhere. Trees next to the half-dozen paths exiting the meadow were denuded of bark. Large piles of bear dung were everywhere. We had inadvertently stumbled into the largest bear kitchen I had ever seen.

Mark was "charge-ahead" nonchalant. He was ready to continue moving upriver in search of elusive steelhead purported to hang among these tens of thousands of spawning Pink and Coho salmon. Nevertheless, I noted his left hand was fondling the 44 magnum bear pistol strapped to his waist. As for me, I was ready to move back downriver to camp, and fast. Bending to my persuasive argument, Mark agreed to retrace our steps back to camp, several miles downstream.

I would later learn that Afognak Island, located just north of Kodiak Island, was purported not only to be home of the largest concentration of Kodiak grizzlies in the world but bears larger than those found on Kodiak Island. Kodiak grizzlies are the largest of all bears, including polar bears. Some individuals weigh well in excess of 1500 pounds. At the time, I was not ready to meet a satiated thousand-pound bear, much less an entire herd of hungry 1500-pounders.

We had been dropped at the Litnik River estuary at the head of Afognak Bay by Seahawk, a Kodiak-based floatplane charter outfit two days previously. According to the pilot, the Coho run was not only the hottest in Alaska but had some of the largest Coho salmon in the world. "Great fishing!" the Beaver pilot informed us at the seaplane dock in Kodiak, "And some great camping spots too. I'd be most happy to fly you there!"

Not once on the dock or during the flight did he mention that great fish runs make great bear habitat. But we were not novices to the Alaska wilderness. Had we thought about it would have guessed. Had I realized the difference I might have responded with, "Yeah, sure. And make meals for a whole herd of giant bears."

As it turned out the Coho fishing was some of the greatest that either Mark or I had ever experienced. We caught incoming Coho in droves at the spot where tidewater pushed the Litnik River. Twelve- to 18-pound dollar-bright Coho wreaked havoc on both our arms and fly rods. When the bushplane set down to pick us up three days later we had truly been fished out.

As for bears, we were not bothered except for one close encounter the second night. Mark got up to noise and found a bear fishing our piece of riverfront. I, on the other hand, slept through the entire episode. Good thing we had our food hung twenty feet up in a Sitka spruce. On our way back the pilot told us that we should not have worried. "Afognak bears are not used to humans. They shy back into the woods." Great comfort, after the fact.

Early in the morning the day after we returned to Kodiak, Mark and I visited road-system rivers we had fished on previous trips. We waded the Russian, American, and Olds in search of Coho. All three rivers were inundated with thousands of Pinks and a few medium sized Coho in the ten-pound range, and a few Chum salmon. But they were also inundated

Mark Salo

The author in Afognak River estuary with a bright Coho salmon, Afognak Island, Alaska.

with local Kodiak Islanders. Well, not really inundated, but crowded in terms of the deserted Litnik River.

We left the Kodiak fish for the locals and hopped our Alaska Air internet special back to Anchorage. I had work meetings scheduled the next morning. Mark had to get back to his salt mines in Poulsbo.

What: Coho salmon
Where: Litnik River, Afognak Island, Alaska accessible
by floatplane or charter boat from Kodiak Island
When: September; an Afognak Island Native Corporation
permit is required for access and camping
Equipment: 8-wt. rod, floating line, fluorescent chartreuse Clousers

*One of our Alaska fishing camps. To avoid bears keep all food items and
waste distant from the camp and suspended well out of reach in trees.*

Kenai Peninsula, Alaska

My fishing buddy and I were heading over Turnagain Pass just past the head of Turnagain Arm. This is a most prominent and beautiful waterscape that extends some 30 miles to the south of Anchorage.

The snow-capped mountains of Turnagain Pass form the northern border of the beautiful Kenai Peninsula then proceed south as the Kenai Mountain Range. The slopes of the Kenai Range feed the head waters of a number of famous salmon rivers. The Russian, Kasilof, and Kenai rivers are the recipients of salmon migrating through the rich waters of Cook Inlet. From spring through fall these and other Kenai Peninsula rivers are the final destination for massive runs of Chinook, Red, Pink and Coho salmon, and steelhead trout.

Cook Inlet, from whence Turnagain Arm emanates, is the namesake of Captain James Cook, the famous eighteenth century Pacific explorer. Cook Inlet wends its way south from Anchorage for some 150 miles. To the west of the inlet, massive volcanoes, including Augustine Island, Iliamna, and the famous Redoubt volcano that so violently erupted recently, stud the skyline. Likewise, Turnagain Arm was named by James Cook and his ship's officers for the difficulty in navigating this glacial silt-filled body of water.

The rivers of the Kenai Peninsula were our destination. We were to meet mutual friend and Kenai resident John Martin for a few days of fishing. John was Manager of Fish and Wildlife Service's Alaska Maritime National Wildlife Refuge. He retired to being a sometime fishing guide and expert on Kenai Peninsula salmon runs. As was our experience in past years, John alluded that this second week of June might afford great fly-fishing for Anchor River and Deep Creek Chinook salmon.

These rivers are about 220 road miles from Anchorage. Seward Highway heads east out of downtown Anchorage and follows Turnagain Arm to the Portage Glacier, then heads south over Turnagain Pass. Kenai Highway takes off from Seward Highway and follows the Kenai River to near its outlet on the shores of Cook Inlet. From the town of Kenai the highway follows the coast south to Anchor River and the terminal town of Homer. The drive is one of the most beautiful in Alaska.

We had some great Chinook fishing where these rivers meet the sea, landing a few fish in excess of twenty pounds. Several stripped us as they ran hundreds of yards back out into Cook Inlet. That was several years ago. Since then the Anchor River June Chinook runs have substantially diminished, presumably to over-aggressive offshore sport fisheries targeting these relatively limited returns. But unlike many areas in the lower forty-eight, the wonderful September Coho salmon runs have held up. Same venue, same flies as for the Chinook.

What: Coho salmon, Chinook salmon
Where: Southern Kenai Peninsula
When: June for Kings, September for Coho – check updated regulations on line for open days
Equipment: 8-wt. rod, floating line, fast-sinking fluorescent chartreuse flies

Kodiak Island, Alaska

A cool and misty dawn heralded a typical Kodiak day. Most mornings on Kodiak Island start this way. Mist or light rain often lasts throughout most fall days. From the bridge crossing the Olds River we could see mint-bright silvers moving in with the incoming tide. The Olds River is located some 20 miles on the island highway south of the town of Kodiak. Lloyd, a New Zealand resident, fastened fluorescent chartreuse Clouser to his leader. This was his first trip to Alaska and his first day on one of half a dozen accessible rivers on the paved-road system. He was nearly bursting at the seams with excitement at the sight of exceptionally large Coho salmon moving into the estuary.

We walked toward the river mouth on an expansive estuary flat criss-crossed by low-tide braids in the river. I moved into position on the south side of one of the braids, Lloyd moved to a spot I suggested just across from me. Several other fly anglers arrived and took up positions along the river hundreds of yards up-river from us. It was not long before a large fish erupted from the water on the end of Lloyd's line.

After about 10 minutes of intense battle, along with coaching from me and several other anglers, he led a fourteen-pound Silver to the bank. I dressed the fish, leaving the head and entrails on the bank. Disposing of fish entrails that would otherwise become part of the local ecology once these salmon spawn and die is common practice on most Alaska waters.

We decided to move on to another spot. It was none too soon. A Kodiak grizzly bear of about 500 pounds appeared at the same spot where Lloyd had landed his fish. It soon discovered the fish entrails I had left and de-voured the lot. The bear then took up a fishing position at the spot where Lloyd had caught his fish not half an hour earlier.

Lloyd Powell dealing with a nice Coho salmon in the Olds River estuary.

This Kodiak bear decided to take up a fishing position in the exact same spot where Lloyd Powell was landing his fish (see above). Lloyd judiciously decided to accede his position on the river.

Lloyd and I had become fishing buddies while working together in the Kingdom of Tonga. Tonga is a South Pacific kingdom of some 165 islands located about 400 miles east of Fiji. Lloyd heralded from Wellington, but also had a Batch on the famous Tongariro River near Lake Taupo on New Zealand's north island. Batch is a New Zealand colloquialism for a cabin or small vacation home. Since I had fished the Tongariro and knew some of the local guides we hit it off.

When our assignments were finished I promised to accompany Lloyd to some of my favorite Alaska fishing waters.

Over the ten days we spent together we fished half a dozen rivers and estuaries, and a couple of lakes, all for silver salmon, with incidental catches of spawning Sockeye, Pink and Chum salmon, and the Dolly Varden char foraging for salmon eggs.

There are six major salmon-bearing rivers on approximately 30 miles of paved road that follows a rugged coastline. These are the Buskin River, Russian River, Salt Creek, American River, Olds River, and Pasagchak River. The estuaries of most of these rivers are immediately below the coastal highway. In addition, there are two lakes where hundreds if not thousands of Coho salmon stage waiting for late-fall freshets to move into the small streams they spawn in. Each estuary, river, and lake has unique characteristics that make for diverse fishing experiences.

All of these rivers harbor very large August to September odd-year Pink salmon runs and smaller even-year runs. The Buskin and Pasagchak rivers have very solid July to August Sockeye runs. All have September to October Coho runs with the Buskin, Olds and Pasagschak premier in numbers and size of fish. There is a relatively small summer Chum salmon run in the Olds River, as well as a few King salmon planted to enhance sport fisheries.

Flies of preference include fluorescent chartreuse and fluorescent pink Clousers. However, the author took a number of salmon in excess of seventeen pounds on a size-8 Green Wheenie. These flies are effective cast downstream in front of visible schools of incoming fish that are moving upstream, then stripped.

Getting to and around the Kodiak road system is easy. Alaska and ERA airlines serve Kodiak out of Anchorage; about a 45-minute flight. Rental cars are available at the airport. There a number of good hotels, numerous bed & breakfast accommodations, and fine restaurants in town.

What: Coho salmon
Where: Kodiak Island road system rivers
When: September to October
Equipment: 8-wt. rod, floating line, bait patterns and fluorescent chartreuse flies

A Coho of about eighteen pounds taken by the author on a size-8 Green Wheenie. Note the sea lice just above the anal fin. Sea lice (Lepeophtheirus salmonis) *are external parasites. Sea lice are actually a crustacean related to planktonic copepods. They die and fall off soon after a salmon enters a river.*

7

Environmental Factors Affecting the Abundance of Salmon and Their Prey

"For if one link in nature's chain might be lost, another might be lost, until the whole of things will vanish piecemeal."

—Thomas Jefferson

While this chapter is not about how or when to fish for salmon, it is of importance to anglers who, by their deep interest in fishing, are also interested in preserving our salmon resource. As a professional biologist it seems appropriate to me that I share observations about some of the factors affecting our salmon fisheries.

Troubled Waters

More than 50 years ago Roderick Haig-Brown, renowned angling author, master salmon and steelhead fly-fisherman, Canadian statesman, magistrate, university chancellor, conservationist, and former logger made another statement that epitomized his view of society and conservation. His statement still applies today.

"It is the history of civilizations that conservationists are always defeated... I think there has never yet been, in any state a conservation government, because there have never yet been a people with sufficient humility to take conservation seriously... Conservation means fair and honest dealing with the future, usually at some cost to the present. It is a simple morality, with little to offset the glamour and quick material rewards of the North American deity, Progress."

In part Roderick Haig-Brown was talking about the decline of salmon runs in the Campbell River, Vancouver Island, on which his home was situated. Pacific salmon populations are only a small fraction of what they once were. With the demand for natural resources from expanding human populations, lack of agreement on how to steward our natural resources, and because of an ever-increasing demand for short-term profits, it appears that future declines in many native salmon populations are not only inevitable, but may be catastrophic.

We are already on the precipice of total collapse of many of the native salmon runs on the West Coast of the United States. As of this writing, book nine populations of Chinook salmon are listed under the Endangered Species Act with the near collapse of the once-prolific Sacramento River Chinook salmon runs. Chinook salmon populations in the Columbia River and in Puget Sound have also been determined by the National Oceanographic and Atmospheric Administration to be highly stressed.

Likewise, Oregon, Northern California, Straights of Georgia and Puget Sound Evolutionary Significant Units for Coho salmon are listed under the Endangered Species Act.

According to the NOAA the most dramatic declines in salmon abundance have occurred over the past several decades. In many cases it does not appear that the rates of decline are decreasing, quite the opposite. However, where feeding and spawning habitats have been sufficiently restored and harvest has been limited, some native salmon runs are rebounding. For example, over the past four or five years, summer-run Chum salmon populations in the Hood Canal branch of the Puget Sound have dramatically recovered. This was due to aggressive efforts by state, local governments, tribes, and private individuals (http://wdfw.wa.gov/fish/chum/chum-5b_1.htm).

Sustainability of Salmon Populations

A Piece of the Pie

Among segments of society there are great economic and socio-cultural drives to maximize the use of natural resources for both personal and corporate gain. This has led to shortages of these natural resources. Such is the case with salmon runs. Both salmon and the watersheds they inhabit have been exploited to the point of seriously affecting numbers of salmon. Whether from commercial fishing, land-use decisions, subsistence fishing, or sports angling, all are part of the equation. We all want a piece of a very attractive pie. However, we cannot sustain that pie unless we change the rules of engagement. These rules might address such things as catch and release and changes in how we manage habitat, harvests, and hatcheries, the three big "H's" of salmon conservation.

Hatchery Management Zones

The use of hatcheries to supplement salmon runs appears to have largely contributed to the extinction of wild spawning salmon. There is the much-touted dilution of wild salmon with hatchery salmon. This has been demonstrated to have greatly reduced the ability of many salmon populations to successfully spawn in the wild. However, the additional establishment of Hatchery Management Zones in Washington and Oregon since the 1960s has also had a large effect on the viability of wild-salmon populations. Hatchery Management Zones lead to the overfishing of wild salmon that are co-mingled harvests with targeted hatchery stocks. This has been a major factor in the extinction of many-wild salmon runs. The practice of deliberate overfishing wild-salmon stocks, some to extinction, to harvest hatchery stocks continues to this day (Wright, 2010).

Maximum Sustainable Yield

In my opinion, one of the great salmon-management faux pas of the past century was how the concept of "maximum sustainable yield" was historically applied. That is calculating allowable salmon harvests with the objective of maintaining natural sustainable salmon production levels. Simply stated, the concept was that only enough returning adults were needed to produce the requisite number of juveniles to maintain runs. This idea has been substantially debunked in recent years. Fisheries scientists now realize that many watersheds that supported large numbers of salmon have depended on these large numbers of salmon for long-term maintenance of these very same salmon runs. There are two inter-related factors: One is stream maintenance and the other is watershed maintenance.

Stream Maintenance

It has been demonstrated by Pacific Northwest fisheries scientists that the nutrients from dead and rotting salmon bodies provide nutrients necessary to produce stream-bottom plants and animals. These small plants and animals are necessary as food for the species of juvenile salmon that are adapted to stay in the stream for up to two years before migrating to sea. Further, it has been demonstrated that the number of dead salmon necessary for this is far more than the number needed to reproduce. This makes biological sense considering the high cleansing rates of many westslope salmon streams.

Watershed Maintenance

The nutrients carried by returning adult salmon back to their watersheds is an important factor in the maintenance of the natural attributes of these same watersheds. As it turns out, in relatively undisturbed watersheds nutrients from decaying salmon carcasses are carried back into surrounding forests and fields in numerous ways, including flooding and by mammals and birds. This transport of nutrients back into watersheds can be important in helping to maintain the trees and other plants that make up healthy watersheds and riparian zones.

Healthy watersheds and riparian zones are critical for maintaining healthy streams. They provide shade and in-stream debris critical for salmon spawning and rearing habitat and they mitigate flooding by holding water. Healthy watersheds release water in a more even manner thereby maintaining relatively constant in-stream water volumes.

Marine Derived Nutrients (MDN) is the term fisheries scientists use for those nutrients supplied by the decaying bodies of spawned-out salmon. The importance of Marine Derived Nutrients was discovered by tracing a nitrogen isotope (N15) predominantly found in marine environments into salmon-bearing watersheds. Amazingly, this nitrogen isotope has been related to both foliage and the spacing and width of growth rings in trees near streams (Quinn, 2005). Also amazing is that it was determined that there appears to be a relationship between tree growth and the concentration of this nitrogen isotope in tree tissues. Nutrients necessary for tree growth are often the very same nutrients emanating from dead and decaying salmon bodies.

Noise and Other Environmental Perturbations

One of the issues with sound that has not been scientifically resolved is the effect of human-caused sound pollution on a variety of marine animals, including salmon. As is becoming more evident from scientific investigations, anthropogenic changes in the ocean soundscape are interfering with normal function of ocean ecosystems. Anthropogenic noise comes from sources like ship propellers, sonar from a variety of sources and including military sonar, pile driving, submarines, and a variety of other sources. Very low frequency sound can travel many miles, and at some frequencies and intensities possibly hundreds of miles, far faster than sound travels in air. Noise is becoming increasingly recognized by scientists as one of the major detrimental environmental stimuli to biota that live in ocean waters.

Environmental perturbations can likely overwhelm salmon senses including sight and sound to the point of affecting salmonid survival.

Environmental Factors Affecting Abundance of Prey Species

The ocean surface film contains contaminants such as PCBs and compounds that cause acidity or are otherwise toxic to the early life stages of ocean plankton. Ocean plankton species are a critical component of the oceanic food chain. Included in the food chain are small animals called zooplankton such as krill.

Other animals further up the food chain that feed on zooplankton at some points in their life stages include small fish and squid. Scientists are now quantifying this decrease in overall productivity of the oceans caused by excessive pollution.

Over-fishing of herring, anchovies, and other prey fish may also be a factor. These, among other species, are critical to maintaining healthy ocean food chains. They recycle ocean nutrients critical for plankton growth, and therefore their own self maintenance. Decline in the populations of prey species on which ocean salmon feed, and also commercially important fish species, could affect salmon populations.

Inshore Habitat

Inshore baitfish habitats include beaches, sub-tidal substrates, and eelgrass beds. Many of these have been greatly altered by human activities. There is also some level of human-caused toxic contamination in the bottoms of almost all of our bays, sounds, and estuaries. These are areas where herring and candlefish spawn, and where other salmon prey species live. This is also where juvenile salmon feed before going to sea.

Armoring of the shorelines by structures, such as rip rap and the above concrete wall, interrupts long-shore sand and sediment transport necessary for replenishing and maintaining healthy beach habitat for juvenile salmon, baitfish, and a myriad of other marine organisms. Note that this beach has "hardened" with cobble as a result. Armoring also causes serious adjacent bank erosion as is evident in this picture.

Eelgrass (Zostera marina) beds, rock-structured beaches, and a number of seaweeds including lettuce (Ulva lactuca) provide ideal forage habitat for salmon. Eel grass is a perennial sea grass, not a sea weed. It is important for stabilizing beach sediments.

Paul Stoll

In Puget Sound shoreline rip-rap and other structures have seriously impeded long-shore transport of the sands and other beach materials critical to the maintenance of ecologically healthy beaches. Dredging, filling, rip-rap and resulting beach erosion have contributed to hardening of intertidal substrates. This, in turn, has eliminated habitat for many species of direct or indirect importance for juvenile salmon sustenance. Natural erosion and deposition processes keep many of these habitats biologically active and diverse. For example, surf smelt require stable sandy areas high in the intertidal for spawning. Likewise, unconsolidated substrates are important candlefish habitat. Many eelgrass beds have disappeared as a result of shoreline development. Herring spawn in eelgrass beds.

Water Quality

Turbidity, changes in fresh and brackish water chemical composition and contaminants from runoff have also taken their toll. Runoff from developed (hardened) areas including roads, driveways and lawns contribute large amounts of petroleum, fertilizers, and other contaminants to adjacent streams, and salt waters. Waste-water from failing septic tanks often enters the salt water. Excessive amounts of deciduous tree leaves from alders along streams where native evergreen trees were cut add excessive fertilizing nitrogen compounds. In aggregate, the above can cause serious pollution problems in our bays and inlets.

The Hood Canal, a large arm of the Puget Sound, is a good example of this type of deterioration. Excessive nutrients have caused large summer marine algae growths. When algae deplete these nutrients, massive algae die-offs result. Oxygen in the water is used-up by bacteria feeding on dead algae. This has been a substantial part of the reason for declines in Hood Canal oxygen levels and subsequent fish kills. Low oxygen levels can seriously affect the survival of baitfish and other marine animal populations.

Harvest

Harvest is a factor in the decline of prey-fish populations. In the past herring in particular have been heavily harvested. This is also the case with anchovies. In addition, seaweeds have been harvested to gather the herring roe deposited on it, as popular as caviar in some Asian countries.

The Future

"There is no final ecological truth. All knowledge is a current approximation, and each addition to that knowledge is but a small, incremental step toward understanding. Not only are ecosystems more complex than we think; they are more complex than we can think."

—Jack Ward Thomas, 1992

We could feel the dampness of spring lingering in the early morning hours, two, maybe three weeks after the passing of the vernal equinox. Sun filtering through massive old-growth Douglas fir and western red cedar brought out brightly colored American goldfinches to feed on huckleberry and salal lining riverside glades. It had only been four months since winter floods had scoured rock-strewn meadows of debris. Early summer had come to the forests and streams of the Pacific Northwest.

Fallen alders crossed the riparian boundaries of old-growth forest. The air hung heavy with the characteristic dusky smell of delicate oyster mushrooms clinging to their decaying trunks. As we made our way over and around dead-falls blocking the anglers trail, I strained to catch glimpses of each section of the river, rushing torrents dominating the soundscape. I was looking for a secret forest shaded pool I had visited in past seasons, a home for fall salmon. Had it survived the winter high water?

My companion and I moved up the bank to follow a ridge, then laterally into the heart of yet untouched Olympic rain forest. As we made our way through thick understory we talked in low voices so as not to disturb the trees. We had heard rumors that salvage loggers were scheduled to cut down the "unproductive" old-growth forest to create a tree farm along this stream.

Salvage? Salvage! Salvage from the very diseases and rot that afflicts the collage of elderly trees nature had destined to provide food and nutrients to the forest floor, eventually succoring new generations of trees—and fish. Salvage for unsustainable jobs, at the expense of a new generation of low-land foresters growing trees where tree farms are most productive.

We wondered how in this day and age *our* own government agencies could let minority economic interests drive the political system to the dire detriment of our natural resources. This was our national forest on the very fringes of Olympic National Park. Access was by tax-funded logging roads.

Yet logging rights given to private companies have cost taxpayers dearly, not to mention loss of irreplaceable natural resources. The amount the U.S. government spent to maintain national forest logging roads alone between 1994 and 1995 to support private timber companies has been on the order of 100 million dollars; many more dollars since then. The amount of this cost borne by those timber companies was zero (*Common Cause*, 1995).

Subsequently, the Clinton administration tried to abrogate this by restricting logging-road construction in national forests. This was followed by the Bush administration's attempt to reverse Clinton policies. In deference to constituents, some politicians often do not realize that nature does not respond to politics, nor do they seem to care.

In both of us heartbreak accompanied memories of pristine runs and pools now exposed to sun long since filled with the silt remnants of steep-sloped logging roads and skid paths. At the same time our hearts filled at the excitement of visiting an old friend, the forest. Like that now-obliterated hole we so fondly remembered, the salmon pool that was our destination today would become our memory tomorrow. What would that memory bring?

We made our way out onto a high bank edge that I knew overlooked my secret pool. When we finally squeezed through the forest to open riverside I was at first surprised, then exhilarated at a sight I did not expect to see. High winter water had filled the pool with pea-sized gravel and golf ball rocks. A pair of native Chinook salmon finned in the gentle current near the tailout. They were remnants of the thousands that had once been there.

Where one pool fills another pool is formed. Such is the changing life of an undisturbed river. This pool was a perfect nuptial bedroom for spawning Chinook salmon.

My companion and I picked up our fly rods and prepared to move on. We wanted to enjoy the forest while there was still time.

As long as the natural resources that sustain salmon populations are more profitable for other purposes than the venture restoration of salmon runs, salmon will continue to take a back seat. But this applies to both fish and human health alike.

You can't separate a healthy planet from a healthy person [author: or healthy fish runs] . . . We have leaders who have got to grow up and face this issue. Without nature, we have nothing."

—Ocean explorer David de Rothschild

The goal is always the same; that is using language as a tactic to demonize government as a means to throttle reform and preserve the status quo for its privileged beneficiaries.

—Joel Connelly, Seattle PI, 12 Dec 2010

Decisions on how we manage our environment need to be based on what we do not know rather than what some people think they know. This is a necessarily conservative approach.

—Richard Stoll, 2002

Appendix I

Salmon Identification and Characteristics

Coho Salmon (*Oncorhynchus kisutch*)

Washington Department of Fish and Wildlife

Coho salmon range from central California to the Alaska panhandle, and areas on the south and west coasts of Alaska. They typically run into streams to spawn late summer to early winter, depending on the run. Coho predominantly spawn in small streams or small tributaries to larger rivers during fall to mid-winter.

Coho eggs hatch in the late winter or early spring after six to seven weeks in the redd. Once hatched, they remain mostly immobile in the redd at the alevin life-stage, which lasts for one to two weeks. Alevin rely on their yolk sac for nourishment and growth. When the yolk sac is completely absorbed the alevin will emerge out of the redd. Young Coho spend one to two years in their natal streams, sometimes spending their first winter in off-channel sloughs before undergoing a transformation to the smolt life-stage. Smolts are generally 100 to 150mm long (four to six inches). Smolts migrate to salt water late March through July. Some fish leave fresh water in the spring, spend summer in brackish estuarine ponds and then migrate back into fresh water in the fall before migrating to sea. Coho salmon live in the salt water for one to three years before returning to spawn. Some Coho will become inshore residents, particularly in the Puget Sound and the Salish Sea. Others will return to spawn during their first year as "jacks".

Coho salmon are not heavily spotted. They have a characteristic white gum line which is a distinguishing feature from the black gum lines found on Chinook salmon. At full maturity Coho run from 3 to 20+ pounds, most often depending on the run, the watershed, and the size they attain before running to sea. For example, the fall Coho return into the Pasagschak River on Kodiak Island typically run twelve to twenty two pounds with an average size of approximately fifteen pounds. The reason for their large size appears to be that the juveniles spend a large part of their pre-saltwater stages in Lake Rose Tead, a large, shallow, and very productive lake. The average size of Pasagschak juveniles running to sea appears to be in the range of four to six inches. This gives them a substantial head start on growth. Running to sea at larger size also increases their survival rate. Conversely, Puget Sound and Hood Canal small-stream Coho often run three to six pounds. Puget Sound and Hood Canal drainages are small, flashy (high, high flows and low, low flows). They are very sterile in terms of nutrients as compared to inland drainage rivers. Juveniles from these streams appear run to salt water in the two-to three-inch range. There are certainly other factors that affect size, including the length of stay in salt water and the productivity of the saltwater environment, during any given migration period.

Washington State Department of Fish and Wildlife has long had a program to create resident populations of Coho by late-releasing hatchery fish in the south Puget Sound. Late-release Coho tend not to migrate to sea. These hatchery fish replace the once large numbers of naturally occurring resident Coho.

Chinook Salmon (*Oncorhynchus tshawytscha*)

Washington Department of Fish and Wildlife

'*Oncorhynchus tshawytscha*': Greek *onkos* (hook), *rynchos* (nose); *tshawytscha* (native vernacular among Alaska and Kamchatka native peoples); the Chinook salmon. One way to recognize Chinook salmon is by their solid-black gum lines. Like most salmon, male Chinook can develop a hook nose in preparation during spawning events. But the hook is often not as pronounced as other species of salmon and most notably chum salmon. Chinook salmon are the largest species of salmon. Some individuals in watersheds like the Kenai River south of Anchorage can run up to nearly 100 pounds with fifty-plus-pound fish common.

Chinook salmon can be found from San Francisco Bay in California to north of the Bering Strait, including the arctic waters of Canada and Russia (the Chukchi Sea) and the entire Pacific coast. Populations occur in Asia as far south as the islands of Japan. In Russia, they are found in Kamachatka and the Kuril Islands. The longest Chinook salmon run is up the Yukon River and into northern British Columbia streams.

Chinook salmon can be separated into three types. These are spring, summer, and fall Chinook obviously depending on when they in-migrate to their spawning streams. Fall-run Chinook are the most common.

Chinook salmon are predominantly main-stem spawners. Juveniles emerge from redds in the early spring, 90 to 150 days after the spawn depending on run timing. They spend twelve to eighteen months in the stream before running to sea on very long ocean migration patterns. Substantially depending on the run-specific characteristics, they spend two to five years at sea before returning to spawn.

Chinook salmon are characterized by heavy spotting on the upper side of the body and tail. They have a characteristic black gum line. Except in special circumstances, Chinook salmon are not normally targeted by saltwater fly anglers. Exceptions might be in locations like the mouth of several Kenai Peninsula rivers, such as the Anchor and the Ninilchick. Resident Chinook also provide exciting incidental catches along Puget Sound beaches like Point no Point, most often at dawn or dusk.

Like with Coho, WDFW created a late-release program so that Chinook will stay in inshore salt waters rather than migrate to sea. This is to augment historically abundant resident Chinook populations. A small percentage of resident males will return to spawn in their first year. These precocious early spawners are called jacks. It appears the progeny from jacks do not produce more jacks in any larger proportion than fish that have spent two to four years at sea.

Chum Salmon (*Oncorhynchus keta*)

Washington Department of Fish and Wildlife

Chum salmon are found in the north Pacific, in the waters of Korea, Japan, the Bering sea, British Columbia, and from Alaska to Oregon in the United States. Chum travel more than 2,000 miles up the Yukon River. The northernmost Chums run up the Mackenzie River from Inuvik, through the Great Slave Lake in the Canadian Northwest Territories, to tributaries originating in northern British Columbia. Mature Chum salmon can run from four to in excess of twenty pounds in size depending on the run and river system.

There are both summer- and fall-run chum, notably in the Hood Canal branch of the Puget Sound. Many Chum salmon runs spawn in small streams just upstream from intertidal zones. Chum fry migrate out to sea from March through July, almost immediately after becoming free swimmers after the alevin stage. They spend one to three years traveling very long distances in the ocean. Chum salmon spawn October to January. Females can lay up to 4000 eggs, which are prized in Asian markets as salmon caviar. In saltwater, Chum are silver in color with few or no spots. As they get closer to their spawning stream they radically change in both shape and coloration. Vertical multicolor stripes along the sides of their bodies are characteristic. Male Chum develop formidable looking canine-like teeth, hence the moniker "dog salmon".

Pink Salmon (*Oncorhynchus gorbuscha*)

Washington Department of Fish and Wildlife

Pink salmon range from the Sacramento River in Northern California to the Mackenzie River in Canada; and in the west from Lena River in Siberia to Korea. Populations in Asia occur as far south as Hondo Island in Japan. Pink salmon characteristically run from two to six pounds, rarely much larger.

Pink salmon have a two-year run cycle. Larger run returns occur every other year. Spawning generally occurs between late June and mid-October. Pink salmon spawn in coastal streams and sometimes longer rivers, and may spawn in the intertidal zone or at the mouth of streams if fresh water is available.

Pinks lay from 1000 to 2000 eggs in a redd. Females fiercely guard their redds until death, which sometimes comes within days after spawning. Eggs hatch from December to February, depending on water temperature. Juveniles emerge from the gravel during March and April and quickly migrate downstream to estuaries. Pinks return to fresh water in the summer or autumn as two-year-old adults. Pink and Chum salmon sometimes interbreed in nature to form the hybrid known as the miko salmon. These hybrids are reproductively sterile.

Pink salmon are bright silver in the salt water and have a distinctly forked tail. As males get close to their spawning destination they develop a humped back. Pink salmon can provide an exciting inshore beach sport fishery during their spawning migrations.

Sockeye Salmon (*Oncorhynchus nerka*)

Washington Department of Fish and Wildlife

Sockeye salmon can be found from the Columbia River and Japan to as far north as the Canadian Arctic. They are also found in Siberia. Landlocked sockeye occur in the Yukon Territory and British Columbia in Canada, and in Alaska, Washington, Oregon, California, New York, Utah, Idaho, Montana, Colorado, New Mexico, and Wyoming.

Sockeye spawn mostly in streams having accessible lakes in their watersheds. Some fish spend as long as four years in freshwater lakes before migrating to the ocean. They spend from one to four years in salt water. Where they infrequently spawn in rivers without lakes, fry move to the ocean soon after hatching. Sockeye that live and reproduce in lakes are called "kokanee". Some runs of Sockeye, and also Kokanee, are known to spawn in shallow water near lake shores.

Sockeye have an elongated, torpedo-shaped body and a bluntly-pointed snout. Their coloration in salt water is bluish-green on the back, silver on the belly, with uniform, shiny skin.

Appendix II

The Science Behind Salmon Perception

Color Perception

Like humans, salmonids have rod and cone cells in their retinas. The retina is the light-perception membranes in the rear of the eyes. Rod cells discern black, white, and gray contrasts. Cones are color receptors. Studies of salmonids have determined there are far more rods than cones. Color perception is therefore limited relative to what humans see. Salmon see blue to ultraviolet better than humans and at the higher frequencies (shorter wavelengths). But they do not see as well as humans in the rest of the visible color spectrum. One single study states that salmonids appear to have specific and limited peaks in color perception for three specific color hues. These limited peak perception wavelengths appear to be at 455 nanometers (blue), 530 nanometers (green), and 625 nanometers (orange) (Mueller, et al. 2008). Another study states a peak for one species of salmon at 522 nm (green) (Nakano, et al, 2005). The table on page 132 demonstrates this. However, considering the in ability of salmonids to see colors like oranges and reds in general, and considering the absorption rates of colors in the water column, it is unlikely that those visual peaks above 455 nm have much significance.

Studies have demonstrated that salmonids show a preference for blue under most background and light-intensity conditions. They also show salmon are able to differentiate between subtle differences of shades of blue. Conversely, salmon sensitivity to red is about ten times lower than blue, then correspondingly less for each of purple, orange, brown, yellow and green in that order. But what they actually see depends on a number of factors, including the frequency (in terahertz) and wavelengths (in nanometers) of the available light, depth, and turbidity of the water.

How salmon perceive white may be a factor in how they respond to prey. Most prey fish have white sides and bellies. White is a mix of the full spectrum of colors. A glass prism will split white light into a rainbow of color precisely following the color spectrum. Likewise rainbows are produced by small droplets of water in the sky that act like prisms to split white light into the color spectrum. It may be that salmon see certain of the component colors in white rather than white, particularly in lower frequencies possibly into the ultra-violet component of white. But this has not been demonstrated.

Color Perception in Salmonids in Very Shallow, Clear Water
There is a striking difference between human and salmon color perception.

Color	Wavelength (nm)	Frequency (THz)	Color Perceptions
Ultraviolet	<200	>1000	Salmon: full range to depth
Violet	450-400	1000	Salmon: full range Humans: full range
Blue	490-450	638	Salmon: limited (455 nm) Humans: full range
Green	560-490	566	Salmon: limited (522-530) Humans: full range
Yellow	590-560	517	Salmon: none Humans: full range
Orange	635-590	484	Salmon: very limited (625 nm) Humans: full range
Red	700-635	428	Salmon: none Humans: full range
Infra-Red	>1000	<400	Salmon: none Humans: none

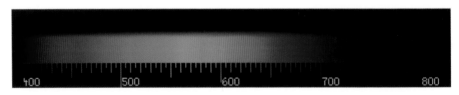

Color spectrum calibrated in nanometers.

In any case, the red side of the color spectrum is not visible below approximately ten feet in depth in clear saltwater and as little as one to two feet in turbid salt water. Light is scattered by particles in turbid water. Greens and then blues increasingly saturate deeper water landscapes with depth to about sixty feet in clear water. The depth of incident light penetration into the water column is also affected by refraction and reflection of light by waves on the surface of the water. Waves refract light into different angles of penetration. The sides of waves reflect more light away from

Depth of Color Penetration in
Clear Ocean Waters (feet)

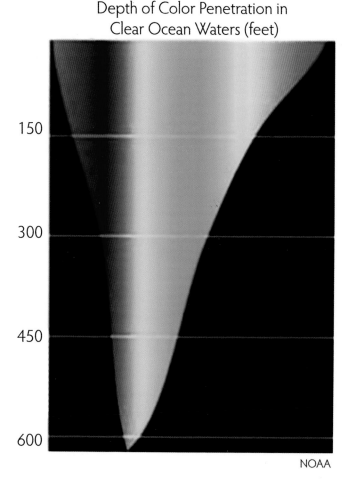

NOAA

the surface of water than in flat water. Therefore, light penetration in rough water is less than in calm water. This results in even faster color attenuation with depth (Ross, 2000).

In near-shore waters that contain high amounts of colored suspended material, the colors that reach the deepest will probably be green and yellow. This is only because more blue light is absorbed at shallower depths, not because green and yellow reach greater depths.

The loss of color not only increases vertically through the water column, but also horizontally. Objects increasingly further away from a fish will appear increasingly colorless and indistinct.

If color is important in deeper water, then flies should be in those lower wavelength hues that given enough light penetration to be visible at depth. These colors are in the blue to ultraviolet range. It makes ecological sense that salmon see best in the blue to ultraviolet color ranges as deeper water landscapes are saturated with these colors.

Studies also show that juvenile salmon and salmon approaching sexual maturity have a higher sensitivity to ultraviolet hues that are below the lowest range of human vision than mid-life salmon (Deutshlander, et al. 2001). During smoltification most salmon lose most of their ultraviolet-sensitive (UVS) cones through programmed cell death. On their return migration back to fresh water, some of these UVS cones are regenerated. Further, salmon that specialize in feeding on plankton (Sockeye, Pinks) also have a higher sensitivity to ultraviolet ranges throughout their adult lives. It has been postulated that this is because many crustaceans and other plankton species smaller salmon feed on reflect ultraviolet hues as a component of their natural coloration.

In some cases, color may not be an issue at all. Salmon most easily observe objects from below. Conversely, salmonids cannot look directly down. The position of their eyes, the shape of their head and mouth parts, and the ovular shape of the eye creates a large down-looking blind spot. Their visual axis is upwards and forward (Nakano, et al, 2005).

It should be noted that salmon eyes are different in terms of how they see when they are in fresh water in both juvenile and spawning adult stages. The light-sensing Rhodopsin-porphyropsin ratios in the rods (not the cones) in the retina change from salt to fresh water favoring porphyropsin. This is an adaptation to accommodate a much brighter environment. Rhodopsin assists fish in object discrimination in the blue to ultraviolet ranges a visual adaption to the darker and deeper waters that salmon experience in saltwater stages and is common in many saltwater species (Toyama, et al., 2008).

The retinal rods and cones in salmonid eyes respond to light and dark with changes in their relative positions. When the light intensity is above the cone thresholds, the eye assumes the light-adapted state; the cone cells contract to be near the source of light while the rod cells elongate into the retina and away from the light. When the light intensity falls below threshold values, the cones expand away from the light source while the rods contract back toward the light. The extent of expansion and elongation is dependent upon ambient light conditions (Ali, 1959, 1979). In functional terms this means that as dark approaches, salmon progressively lose their ability to see color. During bright light conditions they are most sensitive to the colors they can see.

Fluorescence, Phosphorescence, and Bioluminescence

Fluorescence is the emission of electromagnetic radiation by a substance that has absorbed electromagnetic radiation of a different (usually shorter) wavelength. Some very effective flies are tied with fluorescent materials. Fluorescence makes a fly stand out where there is adequate light to make it fluoresce. In most cases, absorption of light, of a certain wavelength induces the emission of light with a longer wavelength (and lower energy). This cannot happen without light such as occurs very early mornings and late evenings, except in the case where shorter wavelength ultraviolet light is being absorbed and then emitted in a longer wavelength.

Studies have shown that fluorescent colors are more visible underwater than the same non-fluorescent colors. Of the fluorescent colors, fluorescent chartreuse is the most visible (Ross, 2000). Chartreuse would normally be increasingly absorbed with depth in the water column. However, fluorescent chartreuse materials absorb shorter wavelength light, including green or blue which are predominant in deeper water landscapes. They then emit light of the longer wavelength, chartreuse, where chartreuse would not otherwise be highly visible. The intensity of light emission from fluorescent chartreuse increases its visibility to fish (Kageyama, 1999).

Phosphorescence is similar to fluorescence in that it is incited by electromagnetic radiation such as light. However, unlike fluorescence, it stores this absorbed energy in a metastable state, releasing it slowly in the form of light. Phosphorescent materials exposed to light will continue to emit light for periods from seconds to months, depending on the material.

Bioluminescence is a completely different phenomenon. Bioluminescence is the emission of light by a chemical reaction in a living organism. A number of phytoplankton species emit light. They appear to depend on this phenomenon for recognition, but also as a flight response to predation. Further, non-luminescent animals may inadvertently become luminescent through contact with bioluminescent plankton.

Sound

Sound, which is caused by pressure waves, is a very significant environmental factor in aquatic environments. The underwater soundscape is diverse, sometimes intense, and can be pervasive. This is especially true in inner sounds and bays where there is a lot of human-caused noise such as boats, pile driving, sonar, and the like.

Sound travels much faster, further, and at much higher sustained intensities in water than in air. Under standard temperature and pressure conditions sound travels approximately 1,100 feet per second in air, but approximately 4,750 feet per second in salt water (about five percent slower in fresh water).

Fish have roughly the equivalent of the human inner ear. Like in humans, the ear functions in both hearing and balance. It is thought that salmonids mostly perceive sound in the lower frequencies. Where the human sound perception is about 20 to 20,000 Hz, salmonids appear to perceive sound in the 10 to 750 Hz range (by avoidance threshold studies). They appear to hear sounds best at less than 150 Hz. These are sub-woofer type frequencies.

Interesting is that while light travels freely through the air/water interface, sound does not. Therefore noise in the air above the water would not

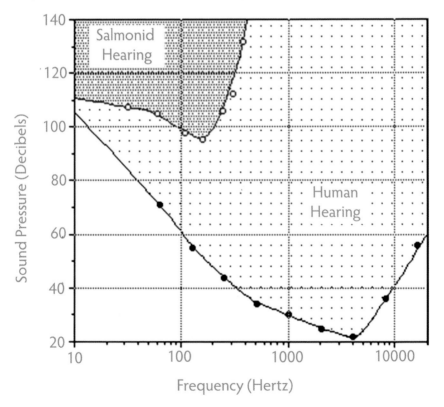

Relative Hearing Ranges; Salmon, Humans (Feist, 1991).

be a large factor in spooking fish, underwater sounds such as pounding on the bottom of a boat could be a very significant factor. So, when fishing out of a boat it's OK to talk loud, but walk softly.

Function of the Lateral Line

Fish perceive the low-frequency pressure waves (100 Hz to less than1 Hz) made by water movement through their lateral lines. Lateral lines are unique in that they combine functional aspects of touch, hearing and seeing. Lateral lines actually function very much like an inner ear. Like ears, lateral lines are located on each side of a fish. Therefore, fish can tell the direction from which these low-frequency waves are coming. Fish can use this sense to a very sophisticated degree. They can detect both large and minute water disturbances, as well as differentiate between different disturbances occurring at the same time.

We are familiar with how waves on the surface of the water fan out in ever increasing concentric circles until they disappear. Likewise, where there are multiple disturbances on the water surface, the waves from each will cross each other. The same thing happens underwater. Lateral lines perceive each of these waves individually and as distinctly different, such as those that might be made by swimming baitfish or schools of baitfish as the case may be.

Salmon can not only perceive small changes in water movements, but the direction from which they come. This is a very useful tool. Salmon can directionally sense prey fish movements to a highly sophisticated degree. They do this to some degree during all feeding periods, but especially in dark conditions and at greater depths where the light is low (Cilia, 2006). As a feeding response mechanism, the lateral line may often be far more important than sight.

Also interesting is how the lateral line assists in low-light navigation around obstructions by detecting water refraction from these obstructions, detect potential predators, and may even assist salmon in finding their way back from deep oceans to their natal streams. For example, deep-ocean navigation by salmon may also be facilitated by magnetic particles (magnetite) that have been detected in the lateral lines of some salmon species.

The Acoustico-Lateralis System

The inner ear and lateral lines form a sensory system that conveys environmental information to the brain of a fish. This includes locating of prey among other things. Where lateral-line organs respond to changes in water pressure and displacement, the inner ear responds to sound and gravity. The inner ear and the lateral lines work both separately and in coordination.

The lateral-line system is a collection of small mechanoreceptive patches or neuromasts located superficially on the skin or just under the skin in fluid-filled canals on the head and body of all fishes. The mechanoreceptive component of the neuromast is the hair cell. This is similar to the sensory cells found in all vertebrate ears, including the human ear. These cells trans-duce mechanical energy into electrical energy when their apical hairs or "cilia" are displaced. The nerves contacting these receptors enter the brain in close association with the auditory-processing areas of the fish's nervous system. Although auditory and lateral-line pathways in the central nervous system are separate, they are largely parallel and share many of the same organizational features, suggesting that the two systems have developed and evolved in close association with each other and may share many of the same attributes.

Potential Effects of Anthropogenic Sound on Salmon

Scientists have recently postulated that "noise pollution" could have serious effects on whale communication. The December 2010 issue of *National Geographic* has a good discussion of this. Likewise, killer whale pods that feed on salmon and other fish often find their prey by echolocation. They do this by bouncing high-frequency sounds off prey. Further, it appears they may even be able to detect the low-frequency vibrations made by swimming fish. Interfering noise pollution could have an effect on their ability to feed, particularly at night and in deeper oceans.

Salmon also have highly sophisticated lower-frequency noise and vibration-detection organs. These include both the inner ears and lateral lines; the acoustico-lateralis system previously described. Considering the pervasive nature of sound in water it is reasonably obvious that these organs are critical for survival by detecting prey, recognizing and avoiding preda-tors, and possibly other critical functions we are not aware of.

While there have been a few studies on salmon avoidance of sound, most of these only address avoidance thresholds or sound barriers. However, sound intensities and frequencies at sub-barrier levels could deleteriously affect salmon in a number of ways. These include interfering with feeding behaviors or even impeding the ability of salmon to effectively feed. There could also be corollary effects on the baitfish salmon feed on.

Appendix III

Prey Species Identification and Characteristics

Pacific Herring

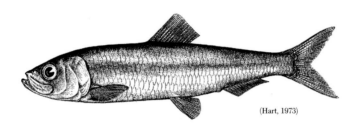

(Hart, 1973)

Pacific Herring (*Clupea harengus pallasi*) are most common summer through fall. In the fall they move to the deeper waters of Puget Sound where they sexually mature. Spawning runs take place from mid-fall to winter when they move up to shallow water to spawn on eel grass or kelp where their eggs stay attached until hatching. A larger species of herring commonly referred to as "horse-herring" can grow to eight inches in length. Horse herring start showing in salmon haunts, including shallow areas along beaches in January. However, the more common smaller herring species show up along beaches, as early as August.

Newly hatched herring will reach an inch or so in length by May. They are three to four inches in length by the commencement of September Coho salmon runs. These yearling herring disappear shortly thereafter, presumably to deep water. Yearlings do not return until their second or third year when they are five to seven inches in length.

Different herring runs are morphologically distinct from each other. Individuals in runs that occur along certain beaches at certain times of the year have somewhat different body shapes and sizes. It is easiest for fly anglers to target runs of smaller herring. Smaller flies are also easier to tie and cast.

Pacific Sand Lance (Candlefish)

Pacific Sand Lance (*Ammodytes hexapterus pallas*), or candlefish as they are locally termed, are ubiquitous throughout inner Puget Sound and many other West Coast inland salt waters. They are also found in a wide range of habitats. Candlefish are important to fly anglers because they occur in abundance along certain sandy beaches in the Straights of San Juan de Fuca and Puget Sound, among other coastal bays and inlets.

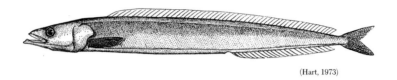

(Hart, 1973)

Candlefish appear along the sandy promontories beginning in June. They can sometimes be so numerous that it is not possible to see the boots of your waders in three feet of clear water. In this case, it is not unusual to see large schools of dogfish (a local shark), ratfish, seals and salmon nearly beaching while gorging on candlefish. But in recent years it seems that candlefish are not quite so abundant.

Surf Smelt

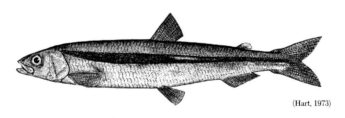

(Hart, 1973)

Surf smelt (*Hypomesus pretiosus pretiosus*) are taxonomically related to salmonids. They rear offshore but make runs into the inner waters of Puget Sound in late summer and early fall. Surf smelt spawn high in the intertidal on calm sandy substrates. Lines of fine broken white shells in sandy high-beach areas are the beach level on which surf smelt often deposit their eggs. Surf smelt disappear soon after spawning. Many hand-net sport fishers target certain beaches to collect buckets full of these fish during their high-tide spawning runs. Sexually mature smelt are considered a delicacy. Although salmon target smelt, because of the limited time they are around they are not as important to anglers as herring and candlefish.

Northern Anchovy

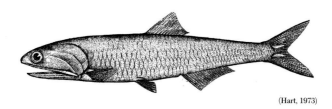

(Hart, 1973)

Just about every predatory fish, bird, and marine mammal on the west coast eats anchovies (*Engraulis mordax*) when they are available. In the Pacific Northwest, juvenile and adult anchovies move into estuaries during spring and summer. They move out during fall. Adults and juveniles also show diurnal movements, especially during the summer, staying at depths of 350-600 feet during the day and coming to the surface at night (McCrae, 1994). This is far too deep for daytime salmon foraging.

There is no doubt that at times northern anchovy are important prey species for Chinook and Coho salmon. However, because of their diurnal behavior they are mostly available as food under dark conditions at night. Because of this, they should rarely be of interest to the inshore salmon fly angler.

Other Prey Species

Salmon opportunistically feed on a variety of marine biota, including small fish and plankton invertebrates. These include crustaceans like crab megalops larvae and other decapods, including a myriad of small shrimp-like animals, and possibly some of the larger copepod species as well. These planktonic species are particularly important to juvenile salmon and salmon that specialize in eating plankton such as Sockeye and Pinks. Megalops larvae are of particular importance to inshore juvenile salmon for food. Female Dungeness crabs will carry as many as 2 million eggs until they hatch into zoea larva. In about a month zoea larvae change into megalops larvae. Megalops can be very abundant drifting throughout inshore marine waters May through September. Mid-summer to early fall they start to settle to the bottom as post-larval crab forms and become unavailable to salmon.

Glossary

Anadromous: Migrating up rivers from the sea to breed in fresh water.

Bioluminescence: Emission of light by a living organism.

Color Spectrum: Range of visible colors between violet and red.

Copepods: Small shrimp-like animals found in plankton.

Crustaceans: Animals with a carapace, such as shrimp and crabs; many small species are found in plankton.

Decapods: Crustaceans (such as shrimps, lobsters, and crabs) with five pairs of thoracic appendages one or more of which are modified into pincers, and with stalked eyes.

Estuary: Body of water into which a river or stream flows.

Ethology: The study of animal behavior.

Euphausids: Krill is the common name for these shrimp-like animals found in all oceans of the world.

Eutrophication: The over-enrichment of water bodies by excessive nutrients, usually caused by human activities.

Evolutionary Significant Unit "ESU": An assemblage of like organisms that are considered distinct for the purposes of conservation. This definition can also apply to sub-species and specific runs of salmon adapted to specific watersheds, as is the case with many native salmon runs.

Galvanic Reaction: An electrochemical process in which one metal corrodes preferentially when in electrical contact with a different type of metal and both metals are immersed in an electrolyte, such as salt water.

Gene Pool: The genetic makeup of an assemblage of organisms that interbreed.

Geo-morphological: Referring to the shape of geological structures; e.g. configuration of the bottom in fishing waters.

Hz (Hertz): Frequency, 1 Hz = one cycle per second.

Invertebrates: Animals without backbones.

Laminar Flow: Unidirectional flow.

Lateral Line: A line bilaterally situated along the length of both sides of fishes that functions in sensory perception of small-water movements.

Marine Derived Nutrients "MDN": Nutrients in streams and watersheds deposited by the decaying bodies of returned salmon.

Megalops Larvae: The planktonic free-floating stage of juvenile crabs.

Metastable: An excited stationary energy state whose lifetime is unusually long.

Morphology: The physical shape of an animal.

Nare: Nasal openings in fish.

Nm (Nanometer): A measure of distance, 1nm = 1 billionth of a meter.

Pelagic: Any water in the sea that is not close to the bottom or near to the shore is in the pelagic zone.

Photophobic: Aversion to light.

Phytoplankton: Very small plant species such as algae suspended in natural bodies of water.

Plankton: Very small plants and animals suspended in natural water bodies.

Redd: A nest created by female salmon by excavating gravel with her tail.

Retina: The sight-perception membrane on the back of the inside of the eye.

Riparian Zone: The vegetated zone next to a river or stream.

Standard Temperature and Pressure: 20 degrees Centigrade at 1 atmosphere pressure (STP).

THz (terahertz): Frequency, 1 THz (terahertz) is one trillion Hertz.

Turbidity: Cloudiness or haziness of a fluid caused by individual particles (suspended solids) like phytoplankton that are generally invisible to the naked eye, similar to smoke in air.

Zooplankton: Very small animal species, such as copepods and megalops larvae, suspended in natural bodies of water.

References

1. Ali, M. A. 1959. **The ocular structure, retinomotor and photobehavioral responses of juvenile Pacific salmon.** *Can. J. Zool.* 37: 965-996.

2. Ali, M.A. 1979. **Environmental Physiology of Fishes.** NATO Advanced Study Institutes Series.

3. Berners, Juliana. 1496. **The Boke of St. Albans.**

4. Common Cause. Fall, 1995. Worldwide Institute. https://www.worldwatch.org/node/782.

5. CILIA-D3.1.3 – public. February 28, 2006. Feasibility Study of Experimentally Establishing Ecological Context for the Lateral Line System.

6. Clouser, Bob and Jay Nichols. January 10, 2006. **Clouser's Flies: Tying and Fishing the Fly Patterns of Bob Clouser.** Stackpole Books.

7. Deutchlander, Mark E, Danielle K. Greaves, Theodore J. Haimberger and Craig W. Hawrshyn. 19 April 2001. **Functional Mapping of Ultraviolet Photosensitivity During Metatrophic Transitions in a Salmonid Fish,** *Oncorhyncus Mykiss*. University of Victoria, British Columbia, Canada.

8. Feist, Blake E. June 1991. **Potential Impacts of Pile Driving on Juvenile Pink (***Oncorhynchus Gorbuscha***) and Chum (***Oncorhynchus Keta***) Salmon Behavior and Distribution.** University of Washington School of Fisheries.

9. Hanneman, Wm., PhD. 2001. **What Trout Actually See. Fly Fishing's Favorite Fable Debunked.** Hanneman Specialties.

10. Hanley, Ken. 2003. **Fly Fishing the Pacific Inshore.** Lyons Press.

11. Hart, J.L. 1973. **Pacific Fishes of Canada.** Fisheries Research Board of Canada, Bulletin 180.

12. Johnson, Les and Bruce Ferguson. 1985. **Fly Fishing for Pacific Salmon.** Frank Amato Publications, Inc. Portland, OR.

13. Johnson, Les and Bruce Ferguson. 2008. **Fly-Fishing for Pacific Salmon II**. Frank Amato Publications, Inc. Portland, OR.

14. Kageyama, Colin J. 1999. **What Fish See.** Frank Amato Publications.

15. Marinaro, Vince, 1976. **In the Ring of the Rise.** Lyons Press.

16. McCrae, Jean. 1994. **Oregon Developmental Species Northern Anchovy,** *Engraulis Mordax.* Oregon Department of Fish and Wildlife.

17. Miyawaki, Leland. 2006. **Puget Sound Beaches: Sea-Runs and Salmon on Poppers.** *Northwest Fly Fishing*, Vol. 8, No 2

18. Mueller, RP and MA Simmons. September 2008. **Characterization of Gatewell Orifice Lighting at the Bonneville Dam Second Powerhouse and Compendium of Research On Light Guidance with Juvenile Salmonids. Final Report.** Prepared for the U.S. Army Corps of Engineers, Portland District, under a Government Order with the U.S. Department of Energy. Contract DE-AC05-76RL01830 Pacific Northwest National Laboratory, Richland, Washington 99352.

19. NAKANO, Norihiko [1]*, Ryo Kawabe [2], Nariharu Yamashita [1], Tomonori Hisrashi [1], Katsutaro Yamamoto [1] and Katsuaki Nashimoto [3]. **Color Vision, Spectral Sensitivity, Accommodation, and Visual Acuity in Juvenile Masou Salmon** *Oncorhyncus Masou Masou.* Graduate School of Fisheries Sciences, Hokkaido University [2] Laboratory of Systematic Fisheries Science, Faculty of Fisheries, and [3] Nippon Data Service, Sapporo, Japan. 2005.

20. Popper, Arthur N. February 21, 2008. **Effects of Mid- and High-Frequency Sonars on Fish.** Environmental BioAcoustics, LLC. Rockville, Maryland.

21. Quinn, Thomas P, 2005. **The Behavior and Ecology of Pacific Salmon and Trout.** University of Washington Press.

22. Railsback, Steven F. [1] Bret C. Harvey, [2] John Hays, [3] and Kirk E. Langory, [3]. 2005. **Tests of Theory for Diel Variation in Salmonid Feeding Activity and Habitat Use.** 1: Lang, Railsback & Associates, Arcata, California. 2: Pacific Southwest Research Station, USDA Forest Service, Redwood Sciences Laboratory, Arcata, California. 3: Environmental Assessment Division, Argonne National Laboratory, Argonne, Illinois, USA.

23. Raymond, Steve, 1996. **The Estuary Flyfisher.** Frank Amato Publications.

24. Ross, Dr. David, 2000. **The Fisherman's Ocean.** Stackpole Books.

25. Ross, Dr. David, Dec 12, 2010. **Midcurrent.** An online magazine.

26. Stoll, R.K., 25 December 2002. **"Preparing for a New Angling Season".** The Kitsap Newspaper Group. Silverdale, WA

27. Stoll, R.K., 2004. **"The Sound of Silver".** Kitsap Newspaper Group Fishing Column, Silverdale, WA

28. Swisher, Doug and Carl Richards, 1971. **Selective Trout.** Crown Publishers.

29. Schweibert, Ernie 1973. **Nymphs.** Lyons Press.

30. Tabory, Lou. 1995. **Saltwater Baits and Their Imitations.** Nick Lyons Publishers.

31. Thomas, Jack Ward. 1992. **Forest Management Approaches on the Public's Lands: Turmoil and Transition.** The Horace M. Albright Lecture in Conservation. College of Natural Resources, University of California, Berkeley.

32. Thomason, Arlen, 2010. **Bugwater.** Stackpole Books.

33. **Tide Log**, Pacific Publishers, Bolinas, CA.

34. Thornton, Barry. 1995. **Saltwater Fly Fishing for Pacific Salmon.** Hancock House Publishers. IBN 0-88839-319-9.

35. Toyama, Mina; Hironaka, Mantaro; Yamahama, Yumi; Horiguchi, Hiroko; Tsukada, Osamu; Uto, Norihiko; Ueno, Yuka; Tokunaga, Fumio; Seno, Keiji; Hariyama, Takahiko. 2008. **Presence Of Rhodopsin And Porphyropsin In The Eyes Of 164 Fishes, Representing Marine, Diadromous, Coastal And Freshwater Species: A Qualitative and Comparative Study[Dagger].** Photochemistry and Photobiology.

36. Wright, Sam. 2010. **Hatchery Salmon Zones.** *The Osprey*, Issue No 66. May 2010.

37. Wulff, Lee. 1939. **Lee Wulff's Handbook of Freshwater Fishing.**

Index

About the Author

Richard Stoll has been a saltwater fly-fisher for nearly 30 years, a fly-angler for more than 50 years. He has published more than 500 articles on sport fishing, outdoors, and environment in newspapers, periodicals, magazines, and books. Richard held an appointment for several years to the Habitat Committee of the Pacific Fisheries Management Council, the organization that oversees offshore USA fisheries between Canada and Mexico.

Richard was a member of the International Game Fish Association (IGFA) International Committee fourteen years running. He represented Washington State, the Kingdom of Tonga, and East Timor.

Richard owned two fly-fishing shops and was a partner in two more fly-fishing shops. His most recent shop was Fly Fishing Magic in Poulsbo, Washington (now Peninsula Outfitters). Richard has also been a Federation of Flyfishers Certified Fly Casting Instructor since near the inception of the program.

Richard is a retired professional Aquatic Biologist and Environmental Engineer. During his international consulting career, Richard has had the opportunity to fish many locations world-wide, including Canada, Mexico, Korea, East Timor, Indonesia, Philippines, New Zealand, Australia, and the Pacific Islands, among other locations.

Richard currently lives in Poulsbo, Washington and fishes Pacific Northwest states, Alaska, with occasional international destinations. He can be reached through his web site, www.westsoundangler.com.

More Popular Saltwater Fly Fishing Books
From Frank Amato Publications

Saltwater Flies:
Over 700 of the Best
by Deke Meyer

SB: $19.95
ISBN-13: 978-1-57188-020-8
UPC: 0-66066-00206-8

Tying Saltwater Flies:
12 of the Best
by Deke Meyer

SB: $9.95
ISBN-13: 978-1-57188-066-6
UPC: 0-66066-00257-0

Fly Fishing for Pacific Salmon II
by Les Johnson and Bruce Ferguson

SB: $39.95
ISBN-13: 978-1-57188-434-3
UPC: 0-81127-00268-9
HB: $59.95
ISBN-13: 978-1-57188-422-0
UPC: 0-81127-00256-6
Ltd. HB: $130.00
ISBN-13: 978-1-57188-423-7
UPC: 0-81127-00257-3

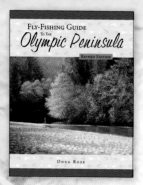

Fly-Fishing Guide to the
Olympic Peninsula
by Doug Rose

SB: $29.95
ISBN-13: 978-1-57188-419-0
UPC: 0-81127-00253-5

Ask for these books at your local fly/tackle shop or call toll-free to order:
1-800-541-9498 (8-5 p.s.t.) • www.AmatoBooks.com